FABRIC
jewellery

FABRIC
jewellery

25 DESIGNS TO MAKE USING SILK, RIBBON, BUTTONS AND BEADS

teresa searle

First published in the UK by
A&C Black Publishers Ltd
36 Soho Square
London W1D 3QY

www.acblack.com

Reprinted 2009

Copyright © 2007 by Breslich &
Foss Ltd

Text by **Teresa Searle**
Photographs by **Lizzie Orme**
Design by **Elizabeth Healey**

**Conceived and produced by
Breslich & Foss Ltd.,**
Unit 2A, Union Court, 20–22 Union
Road, London SW4 6JP

A CIP catalogue record for this
book is available from the British
Library.

ISBN-13: 978-0-7136-8643-2

Printed in China

10 9 8 7 6 5 4 3 2

contents

introduction

In the last few years, designers have increasingly used textile processes and materials to produce beautiful jewellery pieces incorporating texture and colour and bringing a craft aesthetic to high fashion.

Making jewellery from textiles has many advantages: you can create pieces that perfectly accessorise your favourite outfits, choosing colours and embellishments that are personal to you. It can also be an inexpensive hobby, using scraps of vintage fabric, buttons and beads found in charity shops. Pieces made by recycling favourite, but worn out, items of clothing can become highly significant, bringing to mind a happy childhood event, or even a lost love.

As well as indulging yourself, don't forget to make pieces for your friends and family. They will certainly appreciate a handmade present from you, particularly one that has had so much thought put into it. It can also sometimes be quicker to make something at home than to search the shops for the perfect gift.

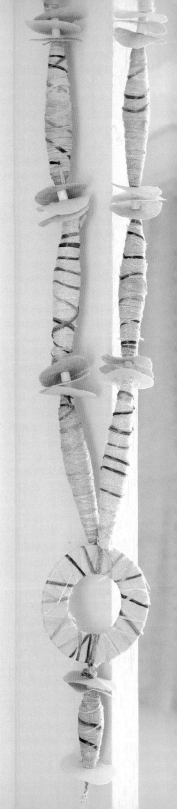

A wide range of pieces is presented here and, in many cases, alternative ideas are also shown to demonstrate the versatility of the process and inspire further ideas. The fabrics used vary greatly from fine, brightly coloured silks and vibrant suedes, to sober linens and vintage cottons. A large range of beads, buttons, braids, ribbons and jewels complements these fabrics to create individual and eye-catching pieces.

The textile processes used include hand and machine embroidery and fabric manipulation, plus a variety of knitted pieces. I hope they will entice the novice maker as well as those with more experience. If you already have sewing and knitting skills, then this book will teach you how to apply them to jewellery making, rather than having to learn a whole new craft from scratch.

All the processes shown are versatile and can easily be customised to suit your personal style. See them as both instructional and inspirational: a guide to applying your own design sense and eclectic materials to making fabric jewellery.

teresa searle

Above: This pretty bracelet is made from buttons sewn onto 1 m (39 in) of suede tape, which is wound around the wrist to produce an eclectic piece of jewellery. A loop is sewn at one end of the tape so the bracelet can be fastened using the first button. See page 54 for instructions.

Below: Instructions for making a vintage corsage can be found on page 61.

CHAPTER ONE
techniques

materials

The materials used in this book vary, but most can be bought from fabric, bead and haberdashery stores. In many cases, materials were sourced from charity shops, as well as relatives' scrap bags and button boxes. Materials themselves can often inspire a project, so collect what you can, live with them and see what emerges in time. Some of the materials that I used have been in my possession for over twenty years, waiting for their time to come. Some projects require specialist materials, so you may need to use the internet to help track these down.

FABRICS

All kinds of fabric can be used in many different ways to make textile jewellery, but most of the projects in the book require fine fabrics, such as silk and viscose chiffon and silk dupion, as these are easily manipulated. Asian fabric stores have a good range of these fabrics, in a gorgeous array of dazzling and subtle colours. Suede scraps can often be bought from artisan leather workers and upholsterers, as well as from craft suppliers. Whole hides can be bought if you plan to make a number of projects or a large number of similar items.

Quilting stores and websites are a great source of pretty, vintage-style floral fabrics. Look for genuine vintage fabrics in charity shops or at the back of your family's wardrobes. Textile and costume dealers often have scraps of vintage fabrics and worn clothing just waiting for a new lease of life.

FABRIC
Clockwise from top left:
suede scraps, silk chiffon, viscose chiffon, habotai silks, vintage fabrics including a vintage embroidered place mat, printed cotton, metallic silk organza, silk dupion.

THREADS

Threads can be used to construct or to decorate your jewellery. For all general stitching, polyester sewing thread is perfect both for hand and machine work. It is useful to use as either a top or bobbin thread when using more expensive embroidery threads.

Embroidery threads come in many types of fibre and quality, including viscose, cotton, linen, silk and wool. Some can be used either for machine or hand embroidery. If you would like to try using a thicker thread on the bobbin of your machine, turn to **Using Thick Threads on The Bobbin** on page 14 for instructions.

As well as your local fabric or craft store, there are many specialist embroidery suppliers offering a wide range of wonderful threads that can bring distinction and interest to your jewellery.

EMBELLISHMENTS

A magpie instinct really pays off when searching for tiny decorative details. It is worth exploring a range of notions and bead suppliers, as they have their secret sources of trinkets from all over the world. Also consider other sources, such as ethnic fabric stores, as well as making use of old jewellery recycled from charity shops.

THREADS
Clockwise from top left: thick viscose machine embroidery threads, polyester threads, fine viscose threads, cotton Perle threads, stranded linen threads.

EMBELLISHMENTS
Clockwise from top left: diamanté stamen, white diamanté stones, Indian sequin motifs, Shisha mirror, stick-on jewels, brads, coloured diamanté stones, flower sequins, enamelled wire, plastic beads, glass beads, turquoise beads, pearl beads. In the centre are Indian flower sequins.

BRAIDS AND RIBBONS

These can either be used in lengths for decorating or wrapping, or individual motifs can be cut off to use as part of an appliqué design. Many fabric and craft shops and haberdashers stock braids and ribbons. Check out specialist stores and suppliers for unusual pieces.

BUTTONS

Buttons are featured in many of the projects in this book. There is a huge variety to be found and I love them for their nostalgic charm. Almost all of the buttons I have used were sourced from vintage and charity shops, as well as my mother's button boxes.

Old mother-of-pearl buttons are easy to find and have so much more personality then their plastic look-a-likes. You will also come across bakelite, casein and plastic buttons from the 30s, 40s and 50s, maybe slightly worn and faded, but great for adding a vintage touch to your work.

JEWELLERY FINDINGS

These are easily available from craft stores and bead suppliers. They are essential in some projects as a means to attach your jewellery to your hair, clothing or body.

BRAIDS AND RIBBONS
Left to right: bias binding, rose motif braids, spotted ribbon, ric-rac, Indian braid, fluted viscose braid.

BUTTONS
Top left and in tin: mother-of-pearl buttons.
Below: casein, plastic and bakelite buttons.

JEWELLERY FINDINGS
Clockwise from top left: hairclip, diamanté and pearl clasp, brooch back, ear wires, headpins, ring mount.

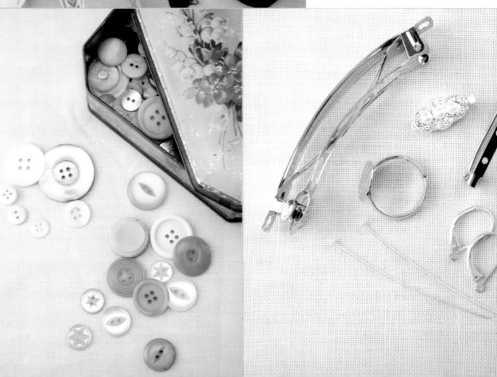

equipment

Most of the equipment used in this book is standard sewing and knitting equipment,

much of which you are likely to have already. Check the individual projects for the

equipment needed before you start them.

Many of the projects require a **sewing machine** for assembly or embroidery. It is helpful to have a machine that can do free machine embroidery for several of the projects, though it is only essential for one of them.

Rotary cutters greatly speed up the process of cutting strips of fabric and are well worth having if you are to make textile jewellery on a regular basis.

Paint palettes are really helpful when beading, as you can arrange your various beads in order as well as having them easily accessible.

I recommend that you invest in a good pair of **embroidery scissors** and that you only use them for fabric and threads so that they remain sharp and reliable.

Fabric glue is used in many of the projects. Choose a strong, white fabric glue that dries clear. This type of glue can also be watered down and used to brush over the surface of fabrics to stiffen them or to make fabric beads.

Quilting pins are great for more unusual textile projects because they are extra-long and have easily visible heads.

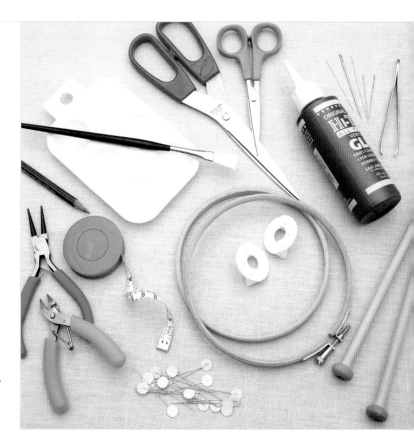

Clockwise from top: paper scissors, embroidery scissors, fabric glue, needles of various kinds and sizes, tweezers, knitting needles, embroidery hoop, pom-pom maker (inside hoop), quilting pins, wire cutters, round-nosed pliers, tape measure, pencil, paintbrush, paint palette.

processes

Each project gives you step-by-step instructions on how to make it, but on these

pages is some general information on the textile processes used.

WORKING WITH SUEDE

With a good strong sewing machine fitted with a leather needle, it is possible to create some interesting pieces of jewellery from off-cuts of suede and leather. You can source these from craft suppliers, artisan shoemakers and upholsterers, as well as by recycling old leather or suede garments. The suede projects in this book would also look great made in felt.

USING THICK THREADS ON THE BOBBIN

In many of the projects, I suggest machine embroidery using a thicker thread on the bobbin and working on the back of the fabric. A stronger, more luxurious line of stitching is made this way, depending on what kinds of threads are used. Viscose and rayon threads are the most commonly available and are used in these projects, but you may also find cotton and wool/acrylic mix threads suitable for this method, too.

If possible, wind the threads onto the bobbin in the normal way using the bobbin winder on your sewing machine. If this is problematic, then wind on the threads by hand. Depending on the thickness of your thread, you may need to adjust the tension screw on your bobbin case to a looser setting (consult your machine manual or a machine specialist).

I recommend that you carry out this task over a box or container of some kind, because if the screw falls out onto the floor, you may never find it again!

Test the stitching on some scrap fabric to check the tension and adjust it again if necessary. When you are working on your project, regularly turn over your work to see how it is progressing.

FREE MACHINE EMBROIDERY

Free machine embroidery is a very useful function and can be used to create a great many effects. It is the nearest thing to drawing with stitch and allows maximum freedom of movement. Check in your manual to see if your sewing machine will do this or consult your supplier: it is referred to as darning on some machines.

In free motion embroidery, the feed dog is lowered and a special presser foot attached (usually it is shorter than a normal foot and is sprung), allowing the fabric to be moved in any direction. Practise the technique on scraps of fabric before attempting a project.

Start by turning the wheel on the end of the machine to lower the needle into the fabric. Slowly press the foot control and, once the

machine has started, move the fabric around, **keeping your fingers well away from the needle**. As the feed dog is no longer there to guide the fabric, your hands have complete control over the movement. Move slowly at first and then practise various lines and movements, such as swirls, to develop your skills.

Once you have become confident, you can run the machine at a faster speed and move the fabric at a corresponding rate. Adjustments may need to be made to the top or bobbin tension and if you find that the thread keeps breaking or is skipping stitches, try using a larger-sized needle. A common mistake is to forget to lower the presser foot and thereby not engage the top tension, resulting in loose uneven stitching and possibly a thread jam under the needle plate.

If your fabric is fine, use an embroidery hoop to hold it taut and ensure it does not pucker up when stitched onto. The hoop can also be used to hold and move the fabric under the needle, meaning that your fingers will not need to go near it. Stiffer fabrics will not need an embroidery hoop, but concentrate on what you are doing and **watch out for your fingers!**

FREE MACHINE EMBROIDERY ON DISSOLVABLE FILM

One of the most interesting ways of using the free machine embroidery process is to stitch onto dissolvable fabrics and films. There are several kinds, but they are all made of a type of fibre or plastic that will dissolve in water.

Build up a network of stitches over the surface of a thick-weight dissolvable film, making sure that each line of stitch is connected with another. (Thinner films will need to be put in an embroidery hoop, but using a thicker-weight film means that you don't need a hoop and have freedom to stitch over a larger area.) Other elements can be incorporated into the embroidery, such as motifs cut from printed fabrics, feathers and fine pieces of plastic.

Once the design is complete, place the embroidery in cold water, then rinse it. The film will dissolve, leaving a stitched filigree fabric that could form the basis of jewellery such as necklaces, chokers, earrings and brooches.

EMBROIDERY ON COVERED BUTTONS

Covering old buttons, or using commercial self-cover buttons, offers a number of opportunities for decoration, including embroidery. Even the smallest remnants of fabric can be decorated with tiny stitches. Using an embroidery hoop will help keep your stitches perfect

and they come in a good variety of sizes to accommodate your assorted scraps of fabric.

Using old buttons is an great opportunity for recycling and is also ideal if you do not want to deal with the shank (common in commercial self-cover buttons). This is particularly useful if you are making brooches, rings or earrings.

WRAPPING AND TYING

Using fabrics to either construct beads or to cover existing objects is a very quick and easy way to create jewellery. You can also customise and update existing pieces in your collection. Ribbons, braids and bias binding can be used to wrap and cover objects, but not to construct beads.

CHAPTER TWO
projects

flower
choker

LAYERS OF CUT OUT SUEDE

flowers, decorated and joined with stitching, are attached to a suede ribbon to make this pretty choker. By making just three flowers you can adapt the idea to make a bracelet, or a single flower will make a brooch or hairclip. As you wear the jewellery it will curl a little, giving it a more naturalistic shape. Check that your sewing machine can cope with three layers of suede. If it won't sew through them all, simplify the design with fewer layers or use the brad technique shown in the Orchid Belt (see page 22).

MATERIALS
- Scraps of suede in pink, red, purple and green
- Machine embroidery thread in lime green
- Polyester sewing thread in pink
- Double-sided adhesive tape
- 1 m (39 in) of suede ribbon or tape (60 cm (24 in) for a bracelet)
- Strong fabric glue

EQUIPMENT
- Template on page 122
- Compasses and ruler
- Card and pencil
- Paper scissors
- Small, sharp embroidery scissors
- Sewing machine
- Leather needle for sewing machine

1 Using the compasses, draw on the card circles with radiuses of 3 cm (1⅛ in), 12 mm (½ in) and 1 cm (⅜ in), and cut them out with the paper scissors. Transfer the flower template onto another piece of card and cut out.

2 Ensuring that you choose a pleasing balance of colours, place the templates on the scraps of suede and draw around them with the pencil to produce two small circles, five medium circles, five large circles and three flower shapes. Cut out all the shapes with the embroidery scissors.

3 Using the embroidery scissors, cut into each large circle from the outside edge towards the centre to form a frayed daisy shape. Make the cuts 5 mm (¼ in) apart and 12 mm (½ in) long.

4 Using double-sided adhesive tape to stick the layers together, make three flowers using a medium circle, a frayed large circle and a flower shape. Make two more flowers using a small circle, a medium circle and a frayed large circle. As you work, make sure you use different colours of suede for each flower and that the flowers will form a good balance of colours across the choker.

4

6

5

5 Thread the sewing machine with the machine embroidery thread on top and the sewing thread on the bobbin. Replace the ordinary needle with the leather needle. Sew stars in the centre of each suede flower. Starting on the outside edge of the inner circle, sew forwards across the centre, then use the reverse function to sew back to the start of the line. Sew forwards again, but this time turn the flower slightly to the right when you reach the centre. Sew across to the far edge of the circle and then reverse again to the other side. Continue in this way until a star has been formed. (It is a good idea to practise this technique on a scrap circle of suede before you start embroidering the flowers.)

6 Arrange the flowers face-down in a line, close together, alternating the two types of flower. Lay the suede tape across the centre, leaving a length at either end for tying. Cut five small circles of suede with a 8 cm (3 in) radius. Apply strong fabric glue to the back of each circle, spreading it out evenly. Stick one to the back of each flower, covering the suede tape, and press firmly. Allow the glue to dry completely before wearing the choker.

MATERIALS

- Scraps of suede in pink, purple, mauve, aqua and green
- Machine embroidery threads in pink, green and aqua
- Polyester sewing threads in toning colours
- Three approximately 2 m (78 in) lengths of suede ribbon or tape, depending on your hip measurement – see Step 5
- Seven flower brads
- Strong fabric glue

EQUIPMENT

- Templates on page 123
- Card and soft pencil
- Paper scissors
- Sewing machine
- Leather needle for sewing machine
- Small, sharp embroidery scissors
- Hole-punch suitable for suede

orchid belt

THIS PROJECT USES SIMILAR TECHNIQUES TO THE

Flower Choker (see page 18), except that the layers are joined with brads, more commonly used in scrapbooking. Brads come in a wide variety of shapes and colours, so search for the ones that will look best in your project. The embroidery thread can be thick machine embroidery thread or buttonhole thread. It is wound onto the bobbin and stitched on the reverse side to produce a prominent effect. Single orchids can be used to make a brooch (see page 25) or a choker.

1 Draw around the petal and leaf templates onto the card. Cut them out with the paper scissors. Place the card templates on the suede scraps and draw around them with the pencil to produce seven of each of the four petal shapes in pink, purple and mauve suede and seven leaves in aqua and green suede. Cut out all the shapes with the embroidery scissors.

2 Wind the embroidery or buttonhole thread onto the bobbin (**see Using Thick Threads on the Bobbin, page 14**). Thread the sewing machine with the embroidery thread on the bobbin and the toning polyester thread on the top.

Set the machine to a long, straight stitch and replace the ordinary needle with the leather needle. Practise the embroidery technique on some scrap pieces before starting the projects as you may need to alter the tension on the top or bobbin threads: consult your manual on how to do this. Working on the back of each suede petal, sew lines in pink thread. In the same way, sew lines up and down the leaf shapes using green and aqua threads.

3 Use the hole-punch to make holes in the petals in the positions shown on the templates.

4 Assemble seven flowers using one of each shape of petal. Lay petal 2 on top of petal 1, aligning the holes, then lay on petals 3 and 4, again aligning all the holes. The orchids work well if petal 3 is a different colour to the other petals. Push a brad through the holes in all four layers, turn the orchid over and split the brad using your fingers, pushing the posts back flat. As you work, make sure you assemble flowers using different shades of suede so they form a good balance of colours across the belt.

variation

Single suede flower motifs can be used to make a brooch. Simply make one flower from either the Orchid Belt or Flower Choker projects. Turn over the flower and cut a circle of suede approx 12 mm (½ in) across. Place the brooch pin onto the back of the flower and stick the suede circle over the mount firmly with some strong fabric glue. Allow to dry thoroughly before wearing.

5 Measure your hips about 5 cm (2 in) below your waist. Cut the suede tape to length, allowing at least an extra 1 m (39 in) for tying. Arrange the orchids face-down and slightly angled in a line that is equal in length to your hip measurement. Lay the suede tapes across the centre of the flowers, close together and making sure 50 cm (20 in) is left at each end for tying. On the right side of each leaf, evenly spread strong fabric glue across the centre section. Stick a leaf to the back of each orchid, covering the suede tape, and press firmly. Allow the glue to dry completely before tying the belt around your hips.

RAID YOUR STASH OF FABRICS, BRAIDS AND BUTTONS
to make a choker or cuff that will complement your personal style.
Here, I have chosen printed silk fabric, rich velvet, braids and old
buttons to create a vintage feel. However, using the same techniques
with different materials – for example, 1970s fabrics, bold buttons and
ric-rac – will create an equally effective choker with a very different
style. To make a matching cuff, use the same instructions but use your
wrist measurements instead. The steps show the cuff, but the choker
follows exactly the same principles.

This design employs free machine embroidery (see Free
Machine Embroidery, page 14). If your machine will
not do this, embroider curving lines using straight stitch in Step 5
instead of free machine embroidery.

vintage
rose cuff and choker

MATERIALS
- Approximately 8 cm (3 in) x 23 cm (9 in) of
  sage-green linen or other stiff fabric for the
  cuff – 8 cm (3 in) x 43 cm (17 in) for choker
- Machine embroidery threads in red and green
- Polyester sewing threads in toning colours
- Scraps of dress fabrics, such as velvet and
  printed silk, in contrasting and toning colours
- Approximately 23 cm (9 in) of braid for the cuff
  – 43 cm (17 in) for the choker
- Motif(s) cut from a piece of braid
- Approximately six vintage buttons in various
  sizes for the cuff – nine for the choker
- Large button for fastening

EQUIPMENT
- Tape measure
- Pencil, paper and ruler
- Paper scissors
- Pins
- Fabric scissors
- Iron
- Sewing machine
- Hand-sewing needle

1 Measure your wrist or neck depending on whether you are making the choker or the cuff. Cut a paper rectangle 8 cm (3 in) wide and the length of your measurement, allowing an extra 6 cm (2½ in) for comfort and for the fastening overlap. Add a 12 mm (½ in) seam allowance all around. Pin the paper pattern to the green linen and cut it out with the fabric scissors.

2 Using the iron, press under the 12 mm (½ in) seam allowance all around. Wrong-sides facing, fold the fabric in half along its length and pin the layers together.

3 Thread the sewing machine with toning polyester sewing thread and set it to straight stitch. Machine sew around the fabric rectangle, sewing approximately 2 mm (¹⁄₁₆ in) in from the edge.

4 Cut small pieces of dress fabrics and arrange them along the linen rectangle, pinning them in place. Leave some areas free to

show the background fabric. Using toning polyester thread and a narrow zig-zag stitch, machine sew the dress fabrics in place around the edge of each piece.

5 Thread the sewing machine with embroidery thread. If you want to use thick threads, wind these onto the bobbin and work from the back (**see Using**

Thick Threads on the Bobbin, page 14). Set the sewing machine to the free machine embroidery function and embroider a random pattern of swirls across an area of the fabric rectangle. Change the thread colours and repeat the pattern. At one end of the rectangle, sew backwards and forwards to create a decorative pattern.

5

6

7

6 Pin the braid in place along one edge of the rectangle. Sew it on using straight machine stitch.

7 Following the instructions in your sewing machine manual, make a buttonhole at one end of the rectangle. Make it approximately 12 mm (½ in) from the edge and a little larger than your chosen button. Hand-sew the fastening button to the opposite end.

8 Using the hand-sewing needle and toning polyester sewing thread, sew the motif in place. Finish by hand-sewing on a number of vintage buttons in a pleasing arrangement.

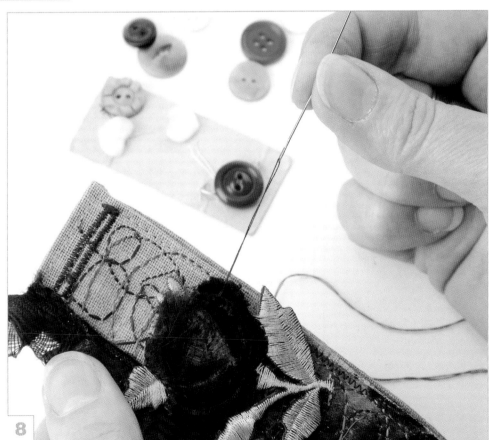

8

KEEP YOUR KEYS HANDY AROUND the house, at work or while out on your bike by hanging them around your neck on this pretty key ribbon. The retro-style ric-rac is put to great effect by sewing it on under one edge of the ribbon to produce a scalloped border.

floral
key ribbon

MATERIALS

- Small scraps of plain, floral and embroidered vintage cotton and linen dress fabrics in toning colours
- Approximately 1 m (39 in) each of jumbo and standard ric-rac in two colours
- Polyester sewing threads in toning colours
- Selection of mother-of-pearl and plastic vintage buttons in various sizes up to 2.5 cm (1 in) across
- Key ring finding

EQUIPMENT

- Pencil, card and ruler
- Paper scissors
- Iron
- Pins
- Fabric scissors or rotary cutter and cutting mat
- Sewing machine
- Hand-sewing needle
- Thimble

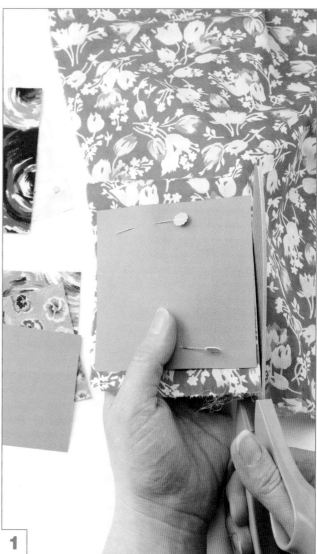

1 Draw two rectangles onto the card, one measuring 10 cm (4 in) square and one measuring 10 x 7.5 cm (4 x 3 in). Cut them out with the paper scissors. Iron your chosen fabrics then pin the card templates onto them. Using the fabric scissors or rotary cutter, cut out a total of 17 pieces, nine of the larger size and eight of the smaller.

2

2 Right-sides facing and aligning the 10 cm (4 in) edges, arrange the pieces to form a long strip, varying the colours, sizes and patterns to best effect. Pin the pieces together. Thread the sewing machine with toning polyester sewing thread and set it to straight stitch. Sew the pieces together, taking a 1 cm (⅜ in) seam allowance. Press the seams flat.

3 Fold the edges into the centre along both sides and press the folds. Fold the fabric strip in half along its length, press the new fold with a hot iron and pin the open edges together.

4

3

5

4 Using the sewing machine and straight stitch, sew along both sides, approximately 2 mm (¹⁄₁₆ in) in from the edges.

5 Decide which side of the fabric length will be the front. Pin the jumbo ric-rac to the back of the fabric ribbon, so that the scalloped edge is just visible from the front. Using the sewing machine and straight stitch, sew it in place, sewing along the middle of the ric-rac. Pin the standard ric-rac to the front of the other side of the

6

7

ribbon, just inside the edge. Sew it in place with straight stitch in the same way.

6 Using the hand-sewing needle and polyester sewing thread, sew the selection of vintage buttons in a pleasing arrangement along the front of the ribbon.

7 Thread the key ring finding onto the fabric ribbon. Fold over 1 cm (⅜ in) at each end of the ribbon, folding one end to the front and one to the back. Place the ends on top of one another, so that the raw edges are concealed and hand-sew them together using overstitch. Slip your keys onto the key ring finding.

MATERIALS

- 28 x 13 cm (11 x 5 in) piece of felt
- Small scraps of silk fabrics
- Machine embroidery threads in colours to complement the fabrics, including thicker threads if you want
- Polyester sewing thread in a toning colour
- Small pieces of braid, ribbon and ric-rac
- Ready-made sequined and embroidered motifs
- Selection of embellishments, such as sequins, small and large beads, sew-on jewels, Shisha mirrors and buttons
- Diamanté and stick-on jewels
- Strong fabric glue
- 28 x 13 cm (11 x 5 in) of silk for lining
- 2.5 cm (1 in) of hook-and-loop fastening
- Decorative button
- 1 m (39 in) of cord

EQUIPMENT

- Card, pencil and ruler
- Paper scissors
- Pins
- Sewing machine
- Fabric scissors
- Hand-sewing needle
- Embroidery scissors
- Thimble

bollywood
iPod case

THE INSPIRATION FOR THIS PROJECT CAME

from watching Bollywood films and from the materials available in Asian fabric stores – a great source of fabrics, sequins and embellishments. This pouch has a felt inner lining and so will help to protect your iPod and its earphones, while the hanging cord will keep the iPod handy around your neck.

1

2

3

4

1 Measure your iPod or MP3 player, including the earphones. Draw a rectangle on the card large enough to accommodate everything with ease and cut it out with the paper scissors. Bear in mind that the fabric can shrink a little when it is embroidered: the example shown measured 10 cm x 13 cm (4 x 5 in). Pin the card pattern to the felt and cut out two pieces using the fabric scissors. Also cut a 2.5 x 6 cm (1 x 2½ in) piece of felt for the fastening strip.

5

2 Cut small rectangles of silk fabrics and pin them to the felt to cover it completely. Cover the fastening strip with one piece of silk.

3 Thread the sewing machine with embroidery thread. Using zig-zag stitch, sew the pieces of silk to the felt, sewing around the edges of each piece.

4 Set the machine to free machine embroidery (**see Free Machine Embroidery, page 14**). Embroider swirling, random patterns over the fabrics, including the fastening strip. If you would like to use thicker threads, wind these onto the bobbin and work on the back (**see Using Thick Threads on the Bobbin, page 14**).

5 Pin lengths of braid to the fabrics. Set the sewing machine to straight stitch and sew on the braid with polyester thread, sewing close to the edges or, for ric-rac, down the centre.

6 Using the hand-sewing needle and polyester sewing thread, embellish the fabrics by sewing on motifs, buttons, sequins, Shisha mirrors and sew-on jewels: remember to decorate the fastening strip, leaving space for the button. Also leave space on the front section at the top centre for the hook-and-loop fastening to be sewn on. Keep all of the embellishments at least 1 cm (⅜ in) away from the edges so that the pieces can be machine sewn together.

6

7 Fill the remaining spaces with diamanté and stick-on jewels using strong glue. Again, leave spaces for the hook-and-loop fastening and machine sewing.

8 Cut out two pieces of lining fabric the same size as the embroidered fabrics. Wrong-sides facing, pin each lining piece to an embroidered piece. Set the sewing machine to satin stitch and, using embroidery thread, sew around the edges of each piece. Line the fastening strip in the same way. Linings facing, pin the two pieces together. Set the sewing machine to zig-zag stitch and, using the same threads used for the satin stitching, sew the pieces together to make a pouch.

9 Pin and hand-sew one end of the fastening strip to the top centre of the pouch on the side that is to be the back. Embellish the other end of the fastening strip with a decorative button. Hand-sew small pieces of hook-and-loop fastening onto the end of the strip (on the lining side) and the front of the pouch to fasten it.

10 If necessary, cut the cord to a suitable length. Tie knots at either end and hand-sew them to the inside edges of the pouch.

7

seed head brooch

THIS PROJECT USES A VARIETY OF FABRICS AND STITCHES
to make a detailed yet subtle brooch. Linen embroidery threads are now available and they are a pleasure to use in this natural-themed piece of jewellery. Choose your largest, flattest button for this project. If you don't have a button large enough, then a circle of stiff mount board will make a good substitute.

MATERIALS
- Flat button at least 4.5 cm (1¾ in) in diameter
- Approximately 15 cm (6 in) square piece of brown dupion silk or other fine fabric – make sure it will fit into your embroidery hoop
- Scraps of fine linen in sage-green
- Scraps of white and grey silk organza
- Stranded linen embroidery threads in sage-green, black and brown
- Polyester sewing thread in a toning colour to the background fabric
- Brooch back finding

EQUIPMENT
- Card, ruler and pencil
- Compasses
- Embroidery scissors
- Pins
- Embroidery hoop
- Fine embroidery needle
- Thimble
- Hand-sewing needle

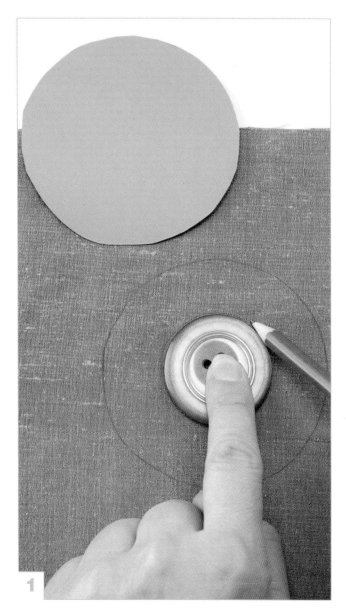

1 Measure the radius of the button and add an extra 2 cm (¾ in). Using the compasses, draw a circle with this radius on the card and cut it out. Place the card circle on the centre of the silk and draw around it with the pencil. Place the button in the centre of the drawn circle and draw around it lightly with the pencil.

2 Using the button as a guide, cut a small strip of linen the diameter of the button and a semi-circle the size of half the button from each colour of organza. Lay one semi-circle on the silk in the inner drawn circle, then place the strip of linen so that it overlaps the straight edge of the semi-circle. Lay the second semi-circle down with the straight edge overlapping the edge of the linen. Pin the fabrics in place.

Stab stitch

Bring the needle and thread up through the fabrics and back down again a short distance away from where they came up, making a small stitch.

3 Place the silk in the embroidery hoop. Using a single strand of sage-green linen embroidery thread and the fine embroidery needle, sew the pieces of organza and linen in place by working small stab stitches around the edges and then randomly all over them.

4 Using two strands of black embroidery thread, backstitch lines to create three upright stems of varying lengths.

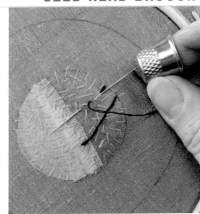

Backstitch

Bring the needle and thread up through the fabrics. Take them back down a short distance to the right, making a small stitch. Bring the needle and thread up again a short distance to the left of the original point. Take them back down through the hole they last came up through to make another small stitch. Continue in this way to make a line of linked stitches.

5 Work several fly stitches on top of one another to create a seed head at the top of one stem, again using two strands of black embroidery thread.

Fly stitch

Bring the needle and thread up through the fabrics. Take the needle down a little to the right of where it came out, but do not pull the thread taut. Bring the needle up again centrally between and a little below the first two points. Slip the loop of thread between the first two points under the tip of the needle and pull the needle and thread taut to make a V shape. Take the needle over the base of the V and down through the fabrics to make a tiny holding stitch.

6 Use detached chain stitch and two strands of black thread to create seedpods along the central stem.

Detached chain stitch

Bring the needle and thread up through the fabrics. Take the needle back down where it came out and bring the tip up through the fabrics a short distance away. Take the thread under the tip of the needle, then pull the needle and thread through to form a loop. Complete the stitch by taking the needle over the end of the loop and down through the fabrics to make a tiny holding stitch.

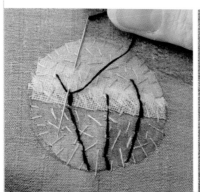

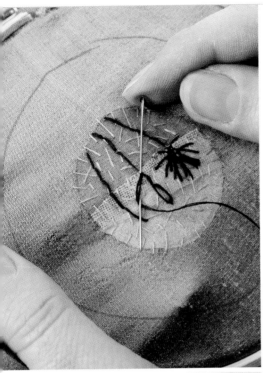

7 Work French knots at the top and down the sides of the third stem to create seeds.

French knots

Bring the needle and thread up through the fabrics. Wind the thread around the needle twice. Take the needle and thread back down where they came out, pulling the knot tight as you do so.

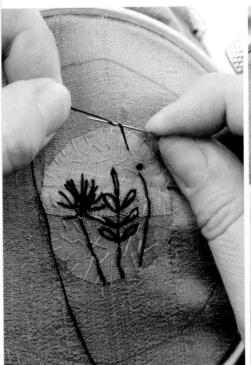

8 Stitch a star at the centre top of the circle of fabrics, using two strands of brown embroidery thread. Fill in remaining unstitched areas with stab stitches and French knots to create randomly placed stems and seeds.

Star stitch

Bring the needle and thread up through the fabric and back down again a short distance away to make a small stitch. Repeat this four times, crossing the stitches to create an eight-pointed star. Finish with two small stab stitches over the centre point – where the larger stitches cross – to hold the star in place.

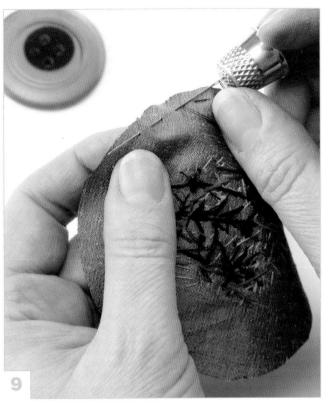

9 Remove the silk from the embroidery hoop and cut out the larger circle. Using the hand-sewing needle and doubled polyester sewing thread, sew a row of small running stitches around the edge of the silk.

10 Lay the button in the middle of the silk circle and pull up the gathers tightly. Make sure the design is centred on the front of the button. Fasten off the thread with several firm backstitches.

11 Out of the remaining silk, cut a circle measuring approximately the same diameter as the button. Turn under 5 mm (¼ in) all around, then pin the circle to the back of the button to cover the gathering. Using small oversewing stitches, sew the circle in place.

12 Hand-sew the brooch back finding to the back of the button, slightly above the centre, using polyester sewing thread and the sewing needle.

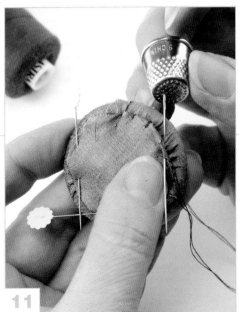

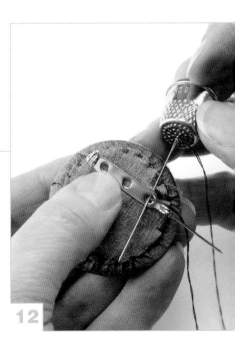

MATERIALS
- Scraps of fine, printed fabrics in a variety of designs
- Six photographs
- Computer printing fabric
- Stranded embroidery threads in toning colours
- Six 2.5 cm (1 in) self-cover buttons
- Polyester sewing thread
- Approximately 64 cm (25 in) of ribbon

EQUIPMENT
- Compasses
- Card and pencil
- Paper scissors
- Pins
- Embroidery scissors
- Computer, scanner and printer
- Embroidery needle
- Hand-sewing needle

childhood memories
bracelet

I AM LUCKY ENOUGH TO HAVE HUNDREDS of images from when my brothers, sister and I were children. I also have a strong memory of my clothes and the fabrics they were made from, helped by my mother's hoard of fabric scraps from every garment she made for us. This bracelet celebrates those times and memories. You can use these ideas to make wonderful presents for family members or as keepsakes for yourself.

This project uses a special fabric product that can be printed on using your computer printer. The fabric is treated with fixative and backed onto paper. When fed through your printer, the fabric will be printed with your selected images. However, you can use more commonly available computer transfer paper to similar effect.

1 Using the compasses, draw a circle on the card with a radius slightly less than twice that of the buttons. Cut it out with the paper scissors. Pin the card template to the printed fabrics and cut out six circles with the embroidery scissors.

2 Scan your photographs, resize and crop them using appropriate software so that the image you want to use is about half the size of the buttons. Save all the pictures in one document so that they can be printed out together. Check the size and quality of the images by printing them onto paper and then print the images onto the fabric, following the manufacturer's instructions.

Cut out the images from the fabric so that they fit inside the circumference of your buttons. Peel off the backing paper.

3 Pin the images centrally or slightly off centre on the fabric circles. Bear in mind that the outside edge of the circle will be underneath the button when it is made up. Carefully sew on the images using the embroidery needle, a single strand of thread and small stab stitches over the edge of the image.

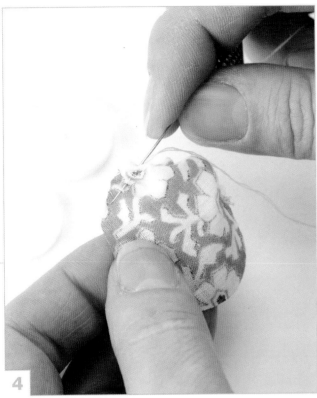

4 Using the hand-sewing needle and doubled polyester sewing thread, sew a row of small running stitches around the circumference of each fabric circle.

5 Place a button inside each circle and pull up the gathers tightly. Make sure the image is correctly positioned over the button. Fasten off the thread using several firm backstitches. Snap the back section of each button into place.

6 Hand-sew the buttons onto a length of ribbon and tie it around your wrist using a double bow.

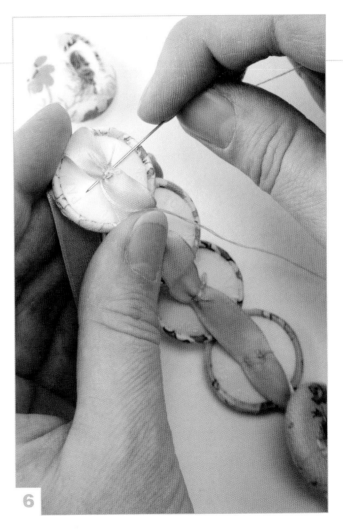

button earrings

RECYCLED BUTTONS AND SILK FROM A HEADSCARF

were used to make these earrings. The embroidery complements the pattern printed on the fabric, embellishing it further. The ring variation on page 55 was made from a tiny scrap of vintage fabric embroidered with French knots to highlight the rose motif.

MATERIALS
- Two 1 cm (⅜ in) buttons
- Scraps of fine, printed fabric with a small pattern
- Embroidery threads in bright colours
- Polyester sewing thread
- Pair of earring stud findings and backs
- Strong glue suitable for fabric and metal

EQUIPMENT
- Soft pencil
- Embroidery hoop
- Embroidery needle
- Thimble
- Small, sharp embroidery scissors
- Hand-sewing needle

1 Place the buttons on selected areas of fabric and draw around them lightly using the soft pencil. Leave at least 2 cm (¾ in) space between the selected areas to allow for cutting out.

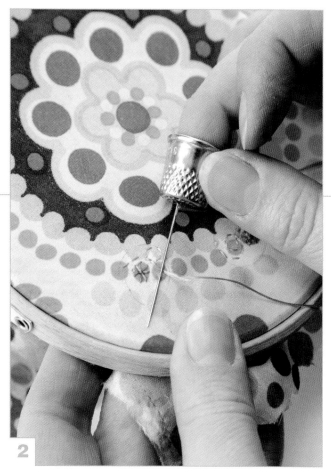

2

4

3

2 Place the fabric in the embroidery hoop. Using the embroidery needle and a single strand of thread, embroider over the printed pattern with a variety of stitches such **French knots and star stitch (see pages 45 and 46)**.

3 Using the embroidery scissors, cut out the circles, cutting 5 mm (¼ in) outside the pencil lines.

4 Using the hand-sewing needle and doubled polyester sewing thread, sew a row of small running stitches around the edges of the fabric circles.

5 Place a button inside each circle and pull up the gathers tightly. Make sure the design is centred on the front of the button. Fasten off the thread using firm backstitches, making the back as flat as possible.

6 Glue earring studs to the back of the buttons and leave to dry.

variation

Here, a small scrap of vintage rosebud fabric was salvaged and embellished with French knots. It was then used to cover a button in the same way as the Button Earrings. The covered button is fixed to a ring mount with strong fabric glue.

COMBINE A SELECTION OF YOUR favourite buttons with ribbon to make a simple bracelet that ties with a bow around your wrist. I made this elegant jewellery piece from a variety of old pearl buttons found in charity, vintage and antique shops.

variation

This bracelet features a collection of marquisate, glass and metal buttons (some of which are Victorian or from my grandmother's button box), sewn onto black velvet ribbon. For an entirely different style, attach multi-coloured buttons to a suede strip, using the same technique as shown here. (See also page 7.)

mother-of-pearl
bracelet

MATERIALS

- Approximately six large mother-of-pearl buttons
- Approximately six medium-sized mother-of-pearl buttons
- Four to six tiny mother-of-pearl buttons
- 65 cm (25½ in) of cream satin ribbon
- Cream polyester sewing thread

EQUIPMENT

- Tape measure
- Pencil
- Hand-sewing needle

1 Lay out the buttons in a pleasing arrangement of styles and sizes, placing small, medium and large ones in piles of two or three and in the order in which you want them on the bracelet. Place the piles in a line, spacing them closely together. Measure the total length of the line and make sure it does not exceed your wrist measurement. Adjust the number or size of buttons accordingly.

2 Cut a length of ribbon the measurement of your wrist, plus 25.5 cm (10 in) at each end for tying. Mark the wrist measurement in the middle section of the ribbon with a pencil.

3 Using the hand-sewing needle and doubled polyester sewing thread, pass the needle through all the buttons in the first pile and sew them onto the ribbon. Make sure the stitches are tight and secure and use all the available holes in the buttons. Fasten off the thread at the back of the ribbon with some secure backstitches. Attach each pile of buttons in this way, making sure each pile touches the last one, until you have covered the length of ribbon marked as your wrist measurement. Tie the ribbon in a bow around your wrist, knotting it twice for security.

suffolk puff
neckpiece

SUFFOLK PUFFS ARE A traditional patchwork technique in which circles of fabric are gathered around the outer edge and then drawn up to create a puff shape. The puffs are sewn together to create a decorative quilt. Here, the same process has been used to create a neckpiece that is embellished further with toning buttons. This neckpiece would also be charming made from a selection of vintage fabrics and buttons, echoing its patchwork origins. If you would like to begin with a less ambitious project, make three puffs into a vintage-style corsage (see page 63).

MATERIALS
- Approximately 33 cm x 1.5 m (13 x 60 in) of each of five gauzy dress fabrics – such as viscose, polyester or silk chiffon – in your chosen colours
- 19 buttons in toning colours and a variety of sizes
- One large button for fastening
- Matching polyester sewing threads

EQUIPMENT
- Compasses
- Card
- Paper scissors
- Pins
- Fabric scissors
- Hand-sewing needle
- Dressmaking mannequin if you have one
- Thimble

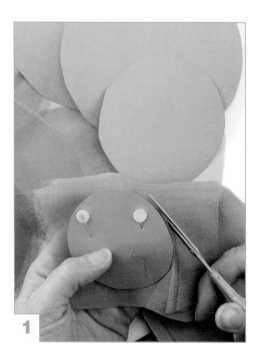

1 Using the compasses, draw circles on the card with the following radiuses: size 1, 9 cm (3½ in); size 2, 7 cm (2¾ in); size 3, 5 cm (2 in); size 4, 4 cm (1½ in). Cut out the card templates with the paper scissors and pin them on the fabrics. Cut out the following circles of fabric, making sure you have a balanced amount of each fabric colour: size 1, cut three; size 2, cut eight; size 3, cut 15; size 4, cut 17. You may wish to fold the fabrics into two or four layers and cut out several circles at the same time.

2 Using the hand-sewing needle and doubled polyester sewing thread, sew a line of running stitches around the edge of each circle, about 5 mm (¼ in) in from the edge. Pull the threads up tightly to create puff shapes. Secure the threads with several oversewing stitches.

3 Build the puffs into groups of two and three as follows: three groups consisting of one each

of sizes 1, 2 and 3; five groups consisting of one each of sizes 2, 3 and 4; six groups consisting of one each of sizes 3 and 4. You should have six very small puffs left over.

4 Lay out the puffs in a circular arrangement with more towards the bottom. If you have a dressmaking mannequin, it is useful to pin the puffs around the neck to assess your composition.

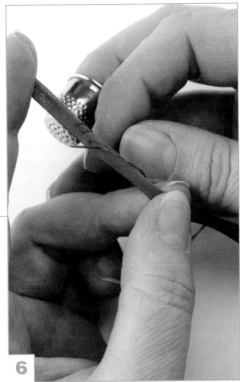

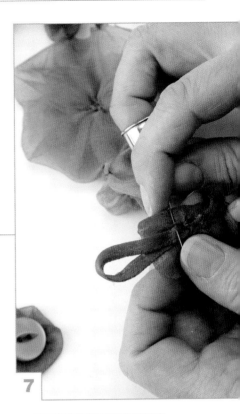

5 Hand-sew the edges of the puffs together with a few small but secure oversewing stitches, following the arrangement set out in Step 4.

6 Cut a strip 12 mm x 10 cm (½ x 4 in) along the selvedge of one of the fabrics. Fold it along its length into three, so that the selvedge is outmost. Overstitch along the edge with polyester sewing thread.

7 Sew the large button to the centre of the last puff on one side. Fold the strip in half and sew the ends to the back of the last puff on the other side, adjusting the length as necessary to accommodate the button.

8 Finally, decorate the centre of each puff by sewing on a button. By leaving this until last you can judge exactly how to arrange the buttons to best effect.

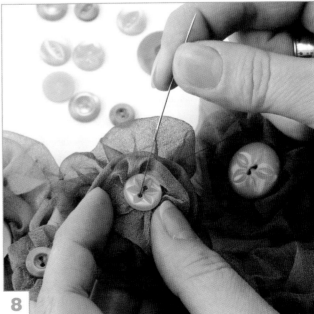

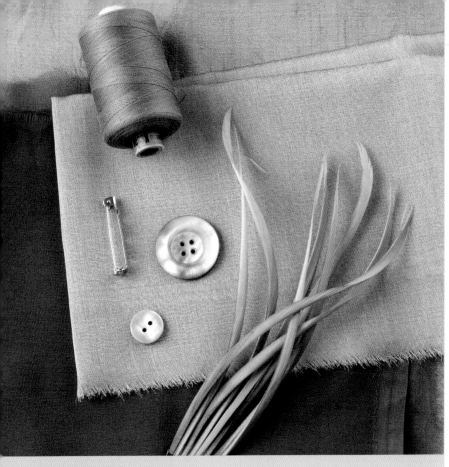

variation

Choose a complementary selection of colours and textures to make a vintage-style corsage. I combined printed rayon curtain fabric with vintage linen. Carefully selected buttons pick up the colours used in the printed fabric.

suffolk puff
corsage

THIS PROJECT USES FEATHERS AS WELL AS SUBTLY

coloured mother-of-pearl buttons to embellish just three puffs.

A larger version could be worn as a fascinator perched on the head

and fastened with a hairclip for a wedding or special occasion.

Also shown is a variation made in printed and plain vintage fabrics

and embellished with a selection of old buttons.

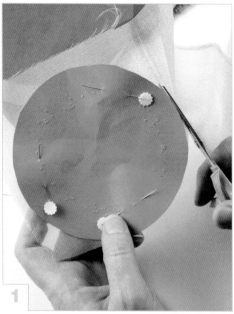

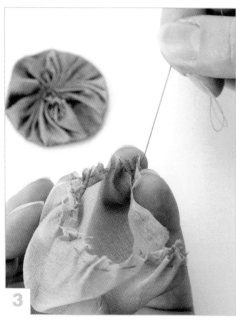

1 Using the compasses, draw circles on the card with radiuses of 8 cm (3⅛ in), 6.5 cm (2½ in) and 5 cm (2 in). Cut out the card templates with the paper scissors. Pin them onto the fabrics and cut out one circle of each size with fabric scissors.

2 Using the hand-sewing needle and doubled polyester sewing thread, sew a line of running stitches around the edge of each circle, approximately 5 mm (¼ in) in from the edge.

3 Pull up the threads tightly to create a puff shape. Secure the threads with several oversewing stitches.

4 Turn over the middle-sized puff and sew the feathers onto the back of it, checking that they form a pleasing arrangement from the front.

5 Place the middle-sized puff on top of the largest one. Place the larger button in the centre and sew the puffs and the button together with several firm stitches.

6 Sew the remaining button to the centre of the smallest puff. Sew the small puff to the side of the largest puff, overlapping the edges. Ensure that the stitches do not show on the front of the work.

7 Using doubled thread and firm stitches, sew the brooch back finding to the back of the corsage.

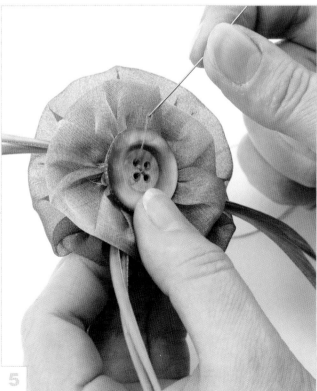

layered
corsage

THIS DELICATE CORSAGE IS MADE BY LAYERING AND then cutting back fine silk fabrics. Fabrics with differing textures, such as chiffons, organzas, habotai and dupion silks, are all appropriate. The centre features a round tassel and a jewel, but you could use a single gorgeous button instead if you prefer.

variations

In the first variation, luscious berry tones were used in a variety of textured silk and viscose fabrics.

A more homely version of the layered corsage can be made with five layers of dotted fabric and a Scottie dog central button. This piece would be perfect for a young girl to wear.

MATERIALS
- 20 approximately 13 cm (5 in) square pieces of fine silk and organza in your chosen colours
- Polyester sewing thread in a toning colour
- Embroidery threads (for the tassel)
- Plastic jewel (for the tassel) or button
- Strong fabric glue (for the tassel)
- Brooch back finding

EQUIPMENT
- Card, ruler and pencil
- Paper scissors
- Pins
- Small, sharp embroidery scissors
- Hand-sewing needle
- Thimble
- Plastic washer (for the tassel)
- Sewing machine (for the tassel)
- Small paintbrush (for the tassel)

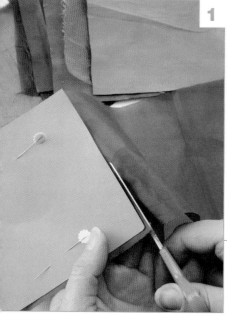

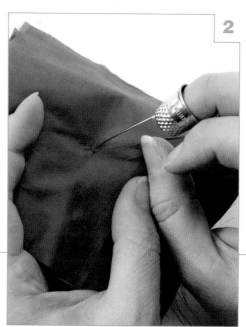

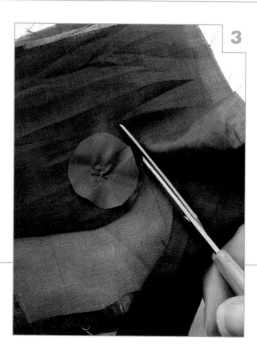

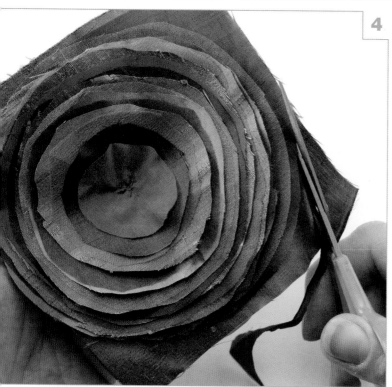

1 Using the ruler and pencil, draw a 13 cm (5 in) square on the card and cut it out with the paper scissors. Use this as a template to cut out 20 pieces from your fabric selection with the embroidery scissors. Your cutting need not be entirely accurate, as you will trim the fabric pieces further at a later stage.

2 Arrange the fabric squares on top of each other, spreading colours and textures evenly throughout the pile. Using the hand-sewing needle and doubled polyester sewing thread, make several stitches through the centre of the pile to hold all the layers firmly together.

3 Using embroidery scissors trim each square into a circle. Start at the top, cutting the first layer back to a tiny circle. As you move down the pile, cut each layer back to make larger and larger circles. (Save the trimmings to make other projects, such as the Rag Flower Corsage on page 72.)

4 Continue trimming until all the layers are revealed and you have a round flower shape.

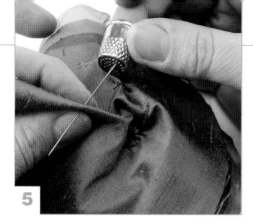

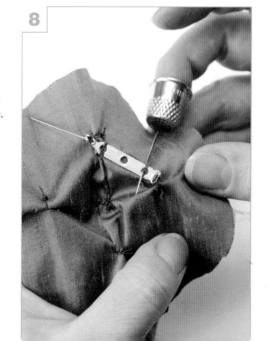

5 Using the hand-sewing needle and polyester sewing thread, work through the layers of the flower a few at a time, tucking and stitching them on the back to create a full flower shape.

6 If you would like to have a round tassel in the centre of the corsage, make one out of embroidery thread, as shown on page 77.

7 Apply glue to the back of the round tassel and stick it to the centre of the corsage. Apply glue to the back of the jewel and stick that in the centre of the round tassel. Allow to dry thoroughly. Alternatively, omit the tassel and sew a button into the centre.

8 Hand-sew the brooch back finding to the back of the corsage, just above the centre.

rose and diamanté
corsage

THIS IS ADAPTED FROM A 1950S
magazine cutting saved by my mother
for many years. Its vintage charm has
been given a kitsch look with the
addition of diamanté stamens. I have made a large and a small rose and placed
them together to wear as a corsage, but there is no reason why you shouldn't make
several roses as a posy for a hat, or even a whole bunch for a wedding bouquet.

MATERIALS

- Two 35 cm (14 in) lengths of paper-coated wire
- Ready-made, wired diamanté stamens
- 40 x 10 cm (16 x 4 in) and 60 x 10 cm (23½ x 4 in) bias strips of pink dupion silk
- 40 x 10 cm (16 x 4 in) and 60 x 10 cm (23½ x 4 in) bias strips of silk chiffon in a similar colour
- Polyester sewing threads in green and pink
- Two approximately 15 cm (6 in) square pieces of green silk organza
- 1 cm x 30 cm (⅜ x 12 in) strip of green silk organza
- Fabric glue that dries clear
- Brooch back finding

EQUIPMENT

- Pins
- Hand-sewing needle
- Template on page 125
- Card and pencil
- Paper scissors
- Thimble
- Fabric scissors
- Wire cutters
- Small paintbrush
- Small container for mixing glue

1

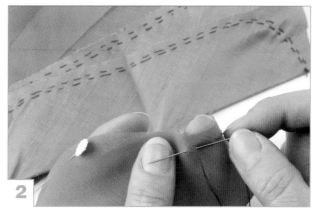

2

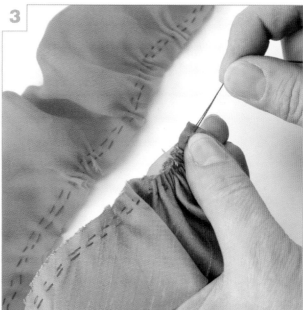

3

1 Fold the lengths of wire in half. Wrap the stamen wires firmly around the loop made in the wires.

2 Fold and pin each strip of dupion silk in half along its length. Using the hand-sewing needle and doubled pink polyester sewing thread, make a double row of running stitch down the short sides and along the bottom edge, curving the lines when sewing around the corners. Cut off the spare fabric around the curved corners.
Repeat this process with the strips of organza.

3 Pull on the threads to gather up each strip to about two-thirds of its original length. To make sure the larger rose is lovely and full, gather the 60 cm (23½ in) strips up a little more tightly than the 40 cm (16 in) strips.

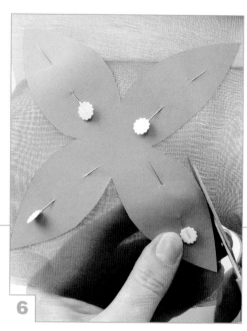

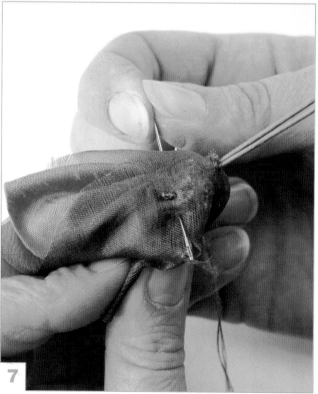

4 Place the larger chiffon strip over the larger dupion strip, adjusting the gathering if necessary to make sure they are the same length. Wind both the strips around the wire at the foot of the stamens.

5 Using the hand-sewing needle, a thimble and the pink polyester sewing thread, secure the wound strips with several firm stitches, passing the needle and thread right through the base of the rose. Repeat Steps 4 and 5 with the shorter lengths of fabric and remaining wire stamen.

6 Transfer the template onto card and cut it out with the paper scissors. Lay the squares of green organza on top of one another. Pin the card template to the fabric and cut out two sets of leaves with the fabric scissors.

7 Push the wire stem of the rose through the middle of one leaf and slide the leaf up to just under the rose. Using the green polyester sewing thread, sew the leaf in position, pushing the needle right through the base of the rose. Attach the other leaf to the smaller rose in the same way.

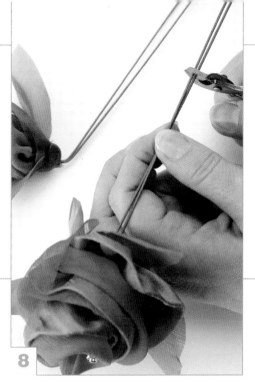

8 Using the wire cutters, trim the stem of the large rose to 10 cm (4 in) from the base of the rose. Bend the smaller rose at a right angle just below its base. Tuck the smaller rose just under the larger and cut the stem so that it aligns with that of the larger rose.

9 Put 1 teaspoon of glue into a container. Add an equal quantity of water and mix together. Paint the diluted glue sparingly onto one organza strip and start to wind it around the stem of the large rose, starting just underneath the base.

10 Place the smaller rose next to the larger one and continue to wind the organza strip tightly around both rose stems. When you get to the bottom of the stems, continue winding back up until the entire strip of fabric is used up. Add more undiluted glue if necessary to hold the strip in place. Allow to dry.

11 Using the hand-sewing needle and green polyester sewing thread, sew the brooch back to the stem.

MATERIALS
- Selection of fine silky fabrics, such as dupion, chiffon and organza, in a variety of colours and textures
- Machine embroidery threads in toning colours, including thicker threads if you wish
- Toning polyester sewing thread
- Strong glue suitable for fabrics and jewels
- Plastic jewel or button
- Brooch back finding

EQUIPMENT
- Small, sharp embroidery scissors
- Rotary cutter and mat (optional)
- Sewing machine
- One 9 cm (3½ in) and one 4 cm (1½ in) diameter plastic washer
- Hand-sewing needle
- Thimble

rag flower
corsage

THESE FLOWERS ARE MADE BY WINDING STRIPS OF stitched fabric around a plastic washer and then stitching the centre to hold the strips together. (Plastic washers are available from hardware stores and builders' merchants.) When the fabric strips are cut, a pretty flower is formed that can be further decorated with threads, buttons and jewels. Develop a habit of collecting both new

and vintage materials for projects like this one that call for a range of fine, silky fabrics. Vintage prints are included in this corsage and in the hair accessory variations page 77.

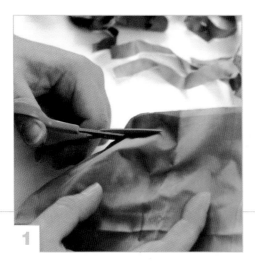

1 Using the scissors or rotary cutter, cut the fabrics into strips about 1 cm (⅜ in) wide and between 12.5 and 15 cm (5 and 6 in) long. You will need about 25 strips to make a corsage.

2 Thread the sewing machine, using a fine rayon thread as the top thread. Wind a thick embroidery thread onto the bobbin (**see Using Thick Threads on the Bobbin, page 14**) or use the same thread as the top. Set the machine to a long stitch length. Sew down the centre of the first strip until you are 1 cm (⅜ in) from the end. Stop the machine and lift the presser foot. Overlap the next strip and continue to sew, joining the strips together. Continue in this way, varying colours and textures, until all the strips are used up.

3 Wind the long strip you have made around the large plastic washer. You need just enough fabric to cover the plastic washer completely, so if the wad in the middle is getting too thick for your machine to cope with, stop winding.

4 Attach a free machine embroidery foot to the sewing machine and drop the feed dog (**see Free Machine Embroidery, page 14**). Being very careful of your fingers, embroider several circles in the centre of the washer, taking care not to sew into the plastic. Alternatively, hand-sew circles into the centre of the flower. Either way, make sure all the strips are sewn together.

5

6

7

8

5 Use the embroidery scissors to cut around the edge of the flower, cutting through all the strips. Remove the plastic washer and tidy up the ends of fabric using the scissors. Choose the best side to use as the front of your flower.

6 Repeat Steps 3–5 using two strands of differently coloured thick embroidery thread on the smaller washer. (If you do not have

a free machine function on your sewing machine, you could make a pom-pom from embroidery thread for the centre of the flower. (**See Cherry Blossom Earrings, page 96**.)

7 Assemble the corsage by gluing the smaller thread flower (or round tassel) into the centre of the fabric flower. Finally, glue a plastic jewel or button into the centre.

8 When the glue is dry, turn over the corsage and sew on a brooch back finding or hair elastic, using the hand-sewing needle and polyester sewing thread. To attach a hairclip finding, glue a circle of fabric over the back of the hairclip and onto the back of the flower.

variation

Use up those remnants of fabric that you can't bear to throw away by transforming them into rag flower hair accessories. These examples are attached to a hairclip finding (front) and a hair elastic (back) and are finished off with matching vintage buttons.

flower
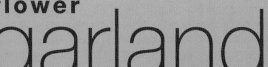
garland

THE FLOWERS IN THIS STRIKING

necklace are constructed using the same simple wrapping process as the Rag Flower Corsage on pages 74–77, but on smaller plastic washers. The cord is made of twisted fabric that is zig-zag-stitched together using machine embroidery threads. An assortment of beads and flowers is then sewn onto the cord. The garland can be made to any length, from a choker to a long-line necklace, by varying the length of the cord and adjusting the number of flowers and beads accordingly.

To make the garland, make five rag flowers and five round tassels. As these will be on a smaller scale, use slightly narrower and shorter strips: 5 mm ($^1/_4$ in) wide and 10–12 cm (4–4$^3/_4$ in) long. You will also need to sew a length of stitched strips 2 m (78 in) long for the cord.

MATERIALS
- Selection of fine silky fabrics, such as dupion, chiffon and organza, in a variety of colours and textures
- Machine embroidery threads in toning colours, including thick threads if you wish
- Toning polyester sewing thread
- Strong glue suitable for fabrics and jewels
- Five plastic jewels
- Approximately 14 large glass or plastic beads in toning colours
- Approximately 100 small glass or plastic beads

EQUIPMENT
- Embroidery scissors
- Rotary cutter and mat (optional)
- Sewing machine
- One 6 cm (2½ in) and one 4 cm (1½ in) plastic washer
- Hand-sewing needle or a beading needle if you use very small beads

1 Assemble five rag flowers as shown on pages 74–77, gluing the two parts of the flower together and adding a jewel or button to the centre. Leave your sewing machine threaded up for use again in Step 3.

2 Take the strip of joined fabrics and fold it in half to make a double strand. Twist one end of the strands tightly.

3 Set the sewing machine to a medium zig-zag stitch. Put the twisted end of the fabric under the presser foot and sew over it to form a cord. Continuing to twist the strands, sew right along their length. (You may need to pull the cord through from the back if your machine is not able to push it through with the feed dog.) Repeat the zig-zag

stitch, using different thread colours on the top spool and bobbin. Join the fabric cord into a loop by sewing the ends together with the machine or by hand.

4 Using the hand-sewing or beading needle and polyester sewing thread, sew a range of toning beads of different sizes along the entire length of the cord, leaving the largest beads until Step 6. Make a firm backstitch after sewing on each bead to ensure that they don't work loose when the necklace is worn, then push the needle through and along the length of the cord to where you want the next bead to be. As you get to the end of a length of thread, secure it with several knotted stitches to prevent the beads working loose.

TIP TO MAKE A SHORTER NECKLACE, SEW ONE END OF THE CORD INTO A SMALL LOOP AND ATTACH A BUTTON TO THE OTHER END. ADJUST THE NUMBER OF FLOWERS ACCORDING TO LENGTH AND PERSONAL PREFERENCE.

5 Sew the flowers onto the cord at about 13 cm (5 in) intervals using the hand-sewing needle and polyester sewing thread. Make sure the cord is not over-twisted at this point and that the flowers naturally fall facing in the same direction. Leave a longer space at the top of the necklace where the cord will go around the back of your neck.

6 Finish the necklace by sewing two or three large beads to the cord between each flower, using the same needle and thread. To attach each bead, make a firm backstitch onto the cord, then thread on a large bead. Thread on a smaller bead, then go back down through the large bead, so the small bead will sit at the top of the hole in the large bead. Make another firm backstitch before pushing the needle through the cord to the next bead position. Make several firm knotted stitches before cutting the thread.

corded
necklace

THIS IS A STUNNING PIECE THAT WOULD BE
wonderful for a special occasion, although it is quite an
investment in time and materials. Strips of fabrics are
fed under the sewing machine to produce cords that
are then embellished with beads of various sizes. I have
chosen a striking colour combination of turquoise and
red and a variety of beads, some of which are genuine
turquoise and bamboo coral.

You could easily reduce the number of strands to
just a few, or even one, to make a simpler necklace, or
make the cords without the beading. A bracelet using
the same process, but shorter strands, or earrings
made from just a few fine strands sewn to ear wires,
will complement the necklace beautifully.

MATERIALS
- Fine fabrics, such as silk dupion and cotton, in shades of two colourways
- Machine embroidery threads, including thick threads for the bobbin, in the same colourways
- Polyester sewing threads in matching colours
- Selection of beads in various sizes and shapes in colours to tone and match the fabrics

EQUIPMENT
- Fabric scissors or rotary cutter and cutting mat
- Sewing machine
- Thimble
- Hand-sewing needle
- Small, sharp embroidery scissors
- Beading needle, if using very small beads
- Dressmaking mannequin if you have one

TIP WHEN WORKING ON A CORDED NECKLACE, IT IS
USEFUL TO HANG THE CORDS AROUND THE NECK OF A
DRESSMAKERS' MANNEQUIN, IF YOU HAVE ONE, TO JUDGE
THE PLACEMENT OF THE BEADS AND THE ORDER IN
WHICH THE CORDS SHOULD HANG.

1

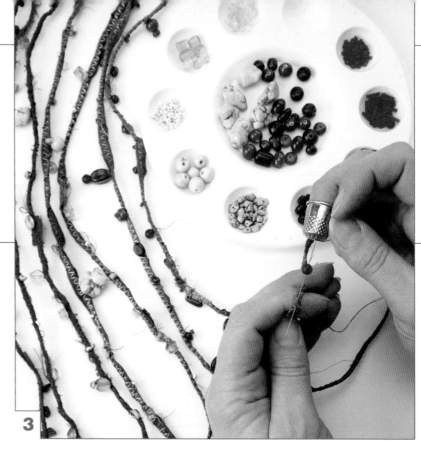

3

2

1 Using the fabric scissors or rotary cutter, cut all the fabrics into strips approximately 1 cm (⅜ in) wide and varying in length from 85 cm to 1 m (33½ to 39 in). You will need ten strips of each colourway, plus an extra one in each colour to bind the strands together.

2 Thread the sewing machine with embroidery threads, putting a thicker thread onto the bobbin if desired (**see Using Thick Threads on the Bobbin, page 14**). Set the machine to zig-zag stitch. Twist one end of a strip and place it under the presser foot of the sewing machine. Sew along the length of the strip, twisting it as you go to form a tight cord. You may have to pull the cord through if it is too narrow for the feed dog to grip. When you reach the end, bring the start of the cord around to meet it, overlap the ends and sew them together to form a loop.

Repeat this process with all the fabric strips, apart from the binding strip. Twist and sew this into a cord, but do not join the ends.

3 Embellish each cord with beads, using the beading needle if necessary and polyester sewing thread. Make a firm backstitch after sewing on each bead to make sure that it stays in place. Leave a gap of 10 cm (4 in) across the join in each cord loop. Ensure that when all the cords are placed together the beads create a good arrangement across the necklace.

A paint palette makes an ideal container in which to keep your beads handy and in order while you bead the cords.

4 Larger beads look better held on by a small bead. To do this, thread the large bead onto the needle, followed by the smaller one.

5 Pass the needle back through the large bead only and make a firm backstitch into the cord.

6 Group together the embellished cords, with all the 10 cm (4 in) spaces aligned. Loop the last 30 cm (12 in) of the binding cord and place it on the bunch of cords, lying in the same direction and with the loop to the left. Working from right to left, wrap the remaining cord tightly around the bunch seven or eight times, leaving at least 5 cm (2 in) of the free end and the loop protruding from the ends of the binding.

7 Thread the end of the wrapping cord through the loop on the left-hand side. Pull the free end on the right hand side so that both the loop and end are pulled through and under the binding. Pull until firm and then trim off the ends of cord close to the binding. Using matching sewing thread, work a few firm stitches at either end of the binding, going through binding and cords for extra security.

filigree
necklace

THIS NECKLACE FEATURES A
variety of flower motifs cut from vintage
and new fabrics and incorporated into a
shaped piece of embroidery worked on
dissolvable film (see Free
Machine Embroidery on
Dissolvable Film, page 15).
Once the film is dissolved, the
embroidery is then further embellished
with mother-of-pearl buttons, pearl beads
and diamanté. These help to add some
weight to the necklace, as well as
making it twinkle and shine irresistibly.

MATERIALS

- 30 x 40 cm (12 x 16 in) of thick, dissolvable film
- A selection of floral vintage-style fabrics with a variety of different-sized motifs
- Approximately 50 cm (20 in) square of medium-weight iron-on interfacing
- Machine embroidery threads in two toning colours, including thick threads if wanted
- Polyester sewing threads in matching colours
- Approximately 12 small mother-of-pearl buttons in various styles
- Approximately nine pearl beads
- Approximately 11 large and 16 medium-sized diamanté
- Strong fabric or gem glue
- Diamanté and pearl clasp finding

EQUIPMENT

- Template on page 124
- Card and pencil
- Paper scissors
- Felt tip pen – not a water-based one, as that will dissolve the film
- Iron
- Small, sharp embroidery scissors
- Sewing machine
- Hand-sewing needle
- Beading needle
- Pins
- Tweezers
- Small paint brush
- Approximately 30 x 40 cm (12 x 16 in) sheet of polythene or plastic

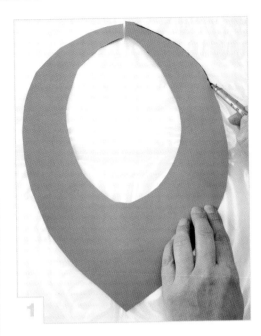

1 Enlarge the template to a size that will fit around your neck and transfer it onto the card. Cut it out with the paper scissors, try it around your neck for size and adjust as necessary. Place the template on the dissolvable film and draw around it using the felt tip pen.

2 Check that the colour of the fabrics and threads you have chosen will not run significantly when wet by dipping small pieces in a bowl of cold water and then pressing them onto a clean white cloth. Choose the motifs you want to use, selecting one large central motif, six medium-sized and five small motifs, but do not cut them out of the fabrics. Place the iron-on interfacing glue-side down on the back of the fabrics, covering the areas of the chosen motifs. Iron the interfacing in

place: this will help to stiffen and support the necklace. Cut out the motifs using the embroidery scissors.

Pin the motifs onto the dissolvable film in a pleasing arrangement. Make sure the pins are in the middle of each motif to avoid them coming into contact with the sewing machine needle.

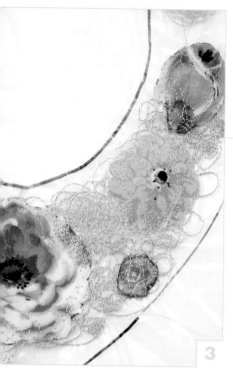

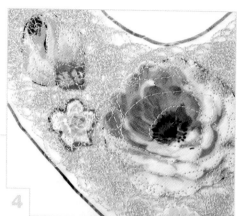

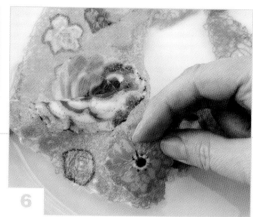

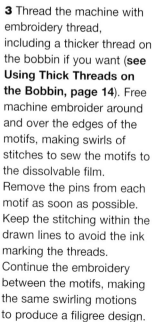

3 Thread the machine with embroidery thread, including a thicker thread on the bobbin if you want (**see Using Thick Threads on the Bobbin, page 14**). Free machine embroider around and over the edges of the motifs, making swirls of stitches to sew the motifs to the dissolvable film. Remove the pins from each motif as soon as possible. Keep the stitching within the drawn lines to avoid the ink marking the threads. Continue the embroidery between the motifs, making the same swirling motions to produce a filigree design.

4 Continue stitching around the whole necklace shape, making small whorls of stitches between motifs to help support the buttons and diamanté. Ensure that all the lines of stitches are connected. They will form a network and keep the piece stable once the film is dissolved.

5 Using the embroidery scissors, cut away any excess dissolvable film around the embroidery, making sure that all the drawn lines are cut away.

6 Soak the embroidery in cold water for a few minutes to soften the film and then rinse it under a cold tap. Keep rinsing until the embroidery no longer feels sticky to the touch. Stretch and reshape the embroidery to fit the original template and lay it flat on the polythene sheet to dry.

7 Using matching polyester thread, sew the buttons and pearl beads onto the embroidery, placing some on the motifs themselves and some on the surrounding filigree. If necessary, use the beading needle to attach the pearl beads, depending on the size of the hole.

8 Dab small spots of strong fabric or gem glue onto the motifs and filigree using the paintbrush. Make sure that they are pleasingly spaced, then apply the diamanté to the glue using the tweezers. Allow to dry on the sheet of polythene or plastic.

9 Cut the embroidery at the centre top point of the necklace. Using matching polyester sewing thread and firm stitches, hand-sew the ends of the clasp to either end of the embroidery.

dahlia
corsage

MATERIALS
- 10.5 x 150 cm (4 x 60 in) of viscose, silk, or polyester chiffon fabric in two colours
- Machine or hand embroidery threads in toning colours
- Scraps of green organza and silk fabrics
- Green polyester sewing thread
- Brooch back finding

EQUIPMENT
- Card and pencil
- Compasses
- Paper scissors
- Templates on page 126
- Fabric scissors or rotary cutter and cutting mat
- Small, sharp-pointed embroidery scissors
- Long darning needle and shorter hand-sewing needle

THE COLOURS,

fabrics and threads used here produce a radiant, dahlia-like pom-pom that makes a real style statement. Vary the size according to your taste and the clothes you want to wear the dahlia with. You can even make a gloriously big corsage from a group of two or three smaller pom-poms with leaves attached. This project uses the traditional method of making pom-poms with card circles, but dedicated pom-pom makers speed up the pom-pom making process enormously.

1 Make a pom-pom template by drawing two circles with a 4.5 cm (1¾ in) radius. Draw a circle with a 2 cm (¾ in) radius centrally inside each larger circle. Cut out the two rings with the paper scissors. Transfer the leaf template onto card and cut it out.

2 Using the fabric scissors or rotary cutter, cut the fabrics into 12 mm (½ in) strips. You will need about five strips, each 1.5 m (60 in) long, of each colour.

3 Place a strip of each colour of fabric together with the same length of embroidery threads. Here I used two fabric colours and four thread colours.

4 Place the card rings together and wind the fabric strips and threads tightly around and through them.

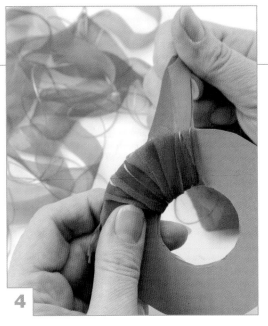

5 Continue winding on strips until the central hole is too small to push any more fabric through.

6 Using the embroidery scissors, cut around the edge of the wound circle, cutting through all the layers of fabric. Make sure the tips of the scissors slip between the card circles to cut the last layers of fabric.

7 Slip four strands of embroidery thread between the card circles and wind them very tightly around the core of fabric. Tie the ends in several firm knots to secure the bundle.

8 Fluff up the pom-pom and trim it a little with the embroidery scissors so that it forms a round ball.

9 Pin the larger leaf template onto the green organza and cut out four leaves. Using the smaller template, cut three leaves from the silk.

10 Arrange the leaves in a fan shape, alternating the fabrics. Using the shorter sewing needle and polyester sewing thread, sew the leaves together about a quarter of the way up from the base of the fan.

11 Using the long darning needle and polyester sewing thread, sew the leaves to the bottom of the pom-pom. Take the needle right through the pom-pom to attach the leaves securely.

12 Hand-sew the brooch finding to the base of the fan of leaves.

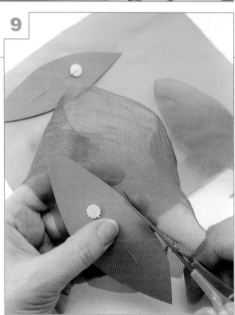

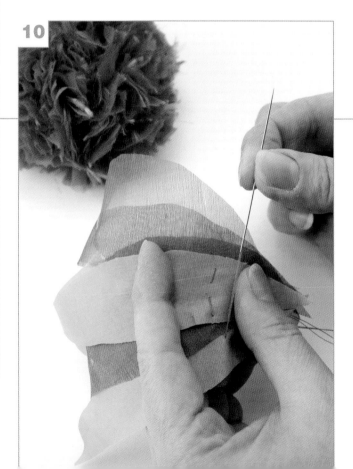

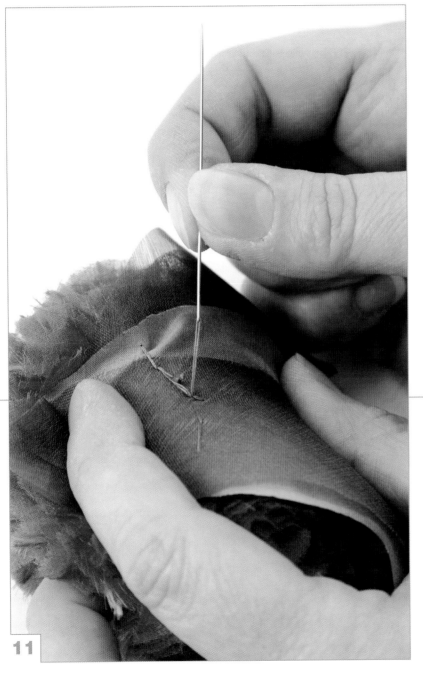

11

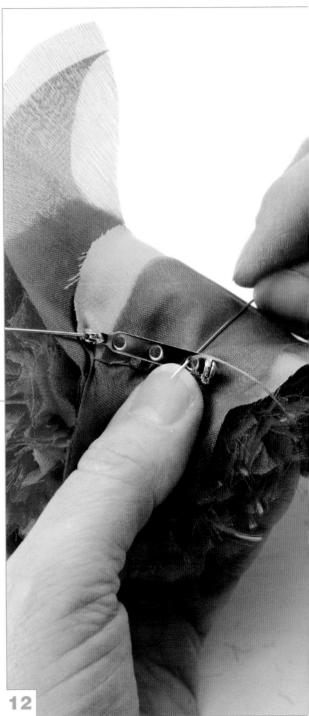

12

THE FINE, PALE-PINK SILK USED TO MAKE these earrings was recycled from a blouse that was destined for the charity shop. Small tufts of thread indicate the flower stamens and the blossoms are finished with leaves made from vintage brocade. The pom-poms are made using a pom-pom maker, but the instructions for using card circles are given if you want to use those instead.

MATERIALS
- Approximately 60 x 8 cm (23½ x 3 in) of pale-pink silk fabric
- Hand embroidery threads in green and pink
- Small scraps of green silk brocade fabric
- Two ear wires
- Two headpins

EQUIPMENT
- Pom-pom maker with 4 cm (1½ in) diameter or small pieces of card, compasses and paper scissors
- Small leaf template on page 126
- Fabric scissors or rotary cutter and cutting mat
- Blunt, large-eyed needle
- Small, sharp-pointed embroidery scissors
- Wire cutters
- Round-nosed jewellery pliers

cherry blossom
earrings

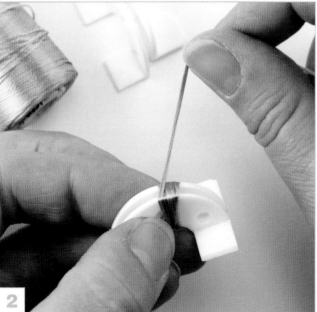

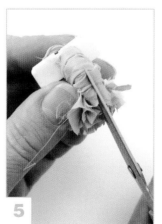

1 If you are using card circles to make the pom-poms, draw the outer circles with 2 cm (¾ in) radii and the inner circles with a 1 cm (⅜ in) radius. Transfer the leaf template onto the card and cut it out.

Using scissors or the rotary cutter, cut the pink silk into 1 cm (⅜ in) strips. You will need eight strips of silk, each 60 cm (23½ in) long, to make two earrings.

2 Wind green embroidery thread around one paired half of the pom-pom maker or card circles: these will form the blossom stamens.

3 Wrap two strips of pink silk around each paired half of the pom-pom maker. If you are using card circles, wrap four fabric strips around and through them. Threading the strips onto a blunt-eyed needle will make this task easier.

4 If using the pom-pom maker, slot the two wrapped halves together, following the manufacturer's instructions.

5 Using the embroidery scissors, cut through the fabric strips around the outside of the wrapped circles, slipping the points between the plastic or card layers.

6

7

8

9

6 Slip a length of pink embroidery thread between the plastic or card layers and tie it tightly around the bundle of fabric strips.

7 Trim the pom-pom a little, but not too much; a slightly untidy pom-pom will give a blousy look perfect for cherry blossom. Make a second pom-pom in the same way.

8 Pin the leaf template onto the silk brocade and cut out four leaves.

9 Push a head pin through the ends of two of the silk leaves: if necessary, make a hole with a large needle first.

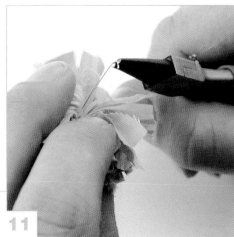

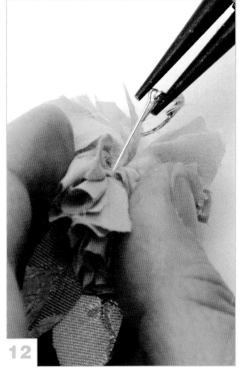

10 Continue to push the head pin through the pom-pom, ensuring that the section of green thread is centre front.

11 Use the wire cutters to cut the wire 1 cm (⅜ in) above the pom-pom. Then use the round-nosed pliers to bend the end of the wire into a small loop.

12 Slip an ear wire onto the loop and squeeze closed with the pliers. Repeat Steps 11 and 12 to make up a second earring in the same way.

THIS NATURAL-TONED NECKLACE

is based on a traditional technique of making beads from rolled strips of paper. Here, paper has been replaced with linen fabric and the beads have been embellished by winding them with raffia threads. You can experiment further with the technique by using different-sized triangles to make larger, smaller or chunkier beads, as well as exploring many different fabrics, textures and wrapping materials.

wrapped necklace

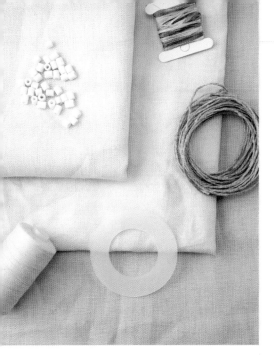

1 Put a little fabric glue into the container and add the same amount of water. Stir thoroughly. Cut a strip of linen 1 x 85 cm (⅜ x 34 in). Using the paintbrush, coat the linen with the diluted glue.

2 Wrap the strip around the plastic washer, holding the end firmly in place at first. Continue to wrap until the whole washer is covered. Make a few stitches with matching polyester sewing thread to hold down the ends of the linen securely.

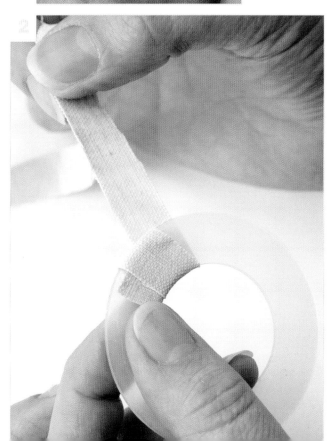

MATERIALS
- White fabric glue that will dry clear
- Selection of linen fabrics of the same weight in three natural shades
- 6 cm (2½ in) diameter plastic washer
- Polyester sewing thread in a matching colour
- Variegated raffia embroidery thread in a toning colour
- Approximately 1.5 m (60 in) of hemp or linen threading cord
- 23 small bone beads in toning colours – the hole must be large enough for the threading cord to pass through

EQUIPMENT
- Small container for mixing glue
- Fabric scissors or rotary cutter and cutting mat
- Small, flat paintbrush
- Hand-sewing needles, including one and with an eye large enough to take the threading cord
- Card, ruler and pencil
- Paper scissors
- Pins
- Fine knitting needle
- Wire rack
- Small, sharp embroidery scissors
- Compasses
- Sheet of polythene or plastic bag

3 Cut a length of embroidery thread at least 85 cm (34 in) long. Wrap this around the washer, spacing the wraps about 5 mm (¼ in) apart. When you have completed the wrapping, tie the ends together with several firm knots. Repeat the process, working in the other direction so that the threads cross each other. Brush a little more diluted glue over the threads to hold them securely in place.

4 Draw two long triangles on the card, one measuring 40 cm (16 in) long with a 9 cm (3½ in) base and the other 45 cm (18 in) long with a 4 cm (1½ in) base.

The length of the triangle will determine how fat your bead is and the base width will determine how long your bead is. Using the paper scissors, cut out the templates.

Pin the shorter template to the linen fabrics and cut out three triangles from each of two colours and four triangles from the third colour, so that you have ten triangles in total. Pin the longer template to one of the fabrics and cut out one triangle.

5 Using the flat paintbrush, paint the diluted glue sparingly onto a shorter fabric triangle.

6 Starting with the widest end, wrap the fabric around the knitting needle.

7 Continue to wind the fabric, keeping the triangular strip as central as possible to create a neat tube bead. Paint the tip of the triangle with un-diluted glue before completing the winding.

8 While the glue is still wet, wrap a length of raffia thread along the bead and back again, so that it crosses itself. Tie the ends together firmly. Brush a little more diluted glue over the thread to hold it in place.

9 Pull the bead gently off the knitting needle and place it on a wire rack. Repeat the process with the rest of the linen triangles to make ten long beads and one shorter, rounder one. Allow the beads to dry overnight in a warm place: the glue should dry clear.

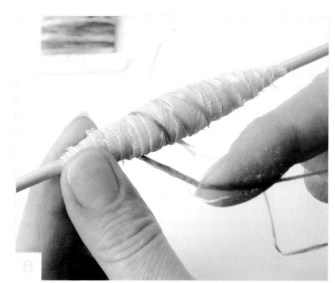

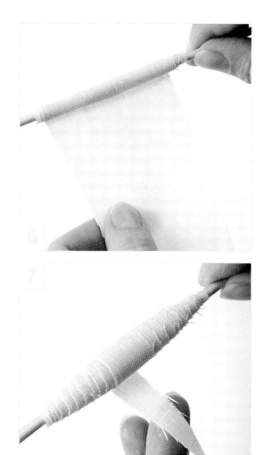

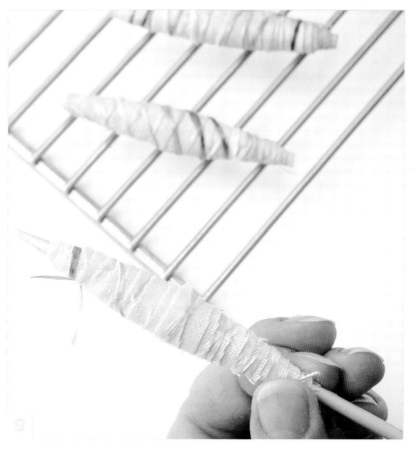

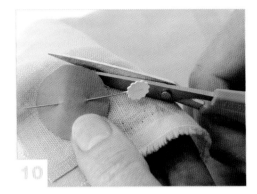

10 Draw a circle with a 12 mm (½ in) radius on the card and cut it out with the paper scissors. Pin the template to the linen fabrics and cut ten from each colour, making 30 circles in total. Paint each circle with diluted glue and leave them to dry on the polythene sheet. The glue will help to stiffen them and prevent them fraying.

11 Cut 30 cm (12 in) of the linen or hemp cord, thread the large needle and knot the end. Thread on a small bone bead, followed by a circle of fabric, the large tube bead, a fabric circle, a bone bead and another fabric circle. Tie the free end of the cord to the wrapped disc with several firm knots and trim off any excess.

12 Fold the remaining length of cord in half. Put the looped end through the wrapped ring, slip the free ends of the cord through the loop and pull tight.

13 Thread a large needle with one end of the cord. Take the needle through one of the tube beads.

TIP USING FABRICS TO CONSTRUCT BEADS OR COVER EXISTING OBJECTS – SUCH AS THE WRAPPED BANGLES ON PAGE 106 – IS A QUICK AND EASY APPROACH TO CREATING NEW JEWELLERY. IT IS ALSO AN INTERESTING WAY TO CUSTOMISE AND UPDATE EXISTING PIECES IN YOUR COLLECTION.

14 Thread on a fabric circle, a bone bead, a circle, a bone bead and another circle. Repeat Steps 13–14 until five long beads have been threaded on, finishing with the fabric circle and bone bead arrangement. Repeat Steps 13–14 on the other free end of the cord. Tie the ends together and trim off any excess cord.

wrapped
bangles

IN THIS PROJECT INEXPENSIVE PLASTIC BANGLES ARE
customised by being wrapped in an assortment of bias bindings
and tapes before being decorated with threads, sequins, buttons
and braids to create an armful of colour. You can also use strips of
printed fabrics and plain and decorative ribbons to wrap bangles.

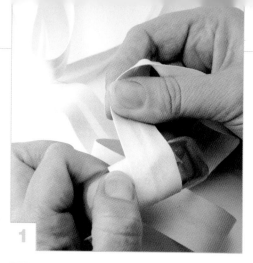

MATERIALS
- Three plastic bangles in various widths – wrapping will make them slightly smaller, so make sure they will be large enough to go over your hand easily
- Approximately 1 m (39 in) of bias binding in each of three colours
- Polyester sewing threads in matching colours
- Approximately 30 cm (12 in) each of ric-rac and ribbon
- Cotton perlé embroidery threads in toning colours
- Fabric glue
- Four buttons in varying sizes
- Beads and sequins in various sizes and toning colours

EQUIPMENT
- Hand-sewing needle
- Small, sharp embroidery scissors
- Small paintbrush
- Beading needle

1 Hold one end of a length of bias binding firmly on the bangle and start to wrap tightly, trapping the end in. Overlapping half the width of the binding with each wrap, cover the whole bangle.

2 Trim off any excess bias binding. Fold over the end of the binding on the inside of the bangle and, using the hand-sewing needle and polyester sewing thread, sew it in place, making sure that the wrapping remains tight.

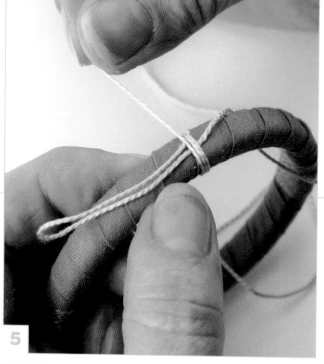

3 Decorate a wide bangle with ric-rac and ribbon. Cut a length of each trim long enough to go around the bangle, plus 1 cm (⅜ in). Using the paintbrush, brush glue along the back of the ribbon and the ric-rac.

4 Stick the ric-rac and ribbon around the bangle in parallel lines. Overlap the ends neatly, press them down firmly and leave to dry.

5 Decorate a narrow bangle with wrapped thread and buttons. Wrap the bangle at four equally spaced points using the cotton perlé embroidery thread. Cut a

50 cm (20 in) length of thread and fold one end over to make a 10 cm (4 in) loop. Lay the loop on the bangle so that it is parallel with it, with the loop pointing to the left. From right to left, wrap the thread around the bangle for about 1–2 cm (⅜–¾ in).

6 Thread the free end through the loop then pull the end to the right so that the loop and the end going through it are pulled under the wrapping. Ensure the wrapping is firm before cutting off the excess ends of thread.

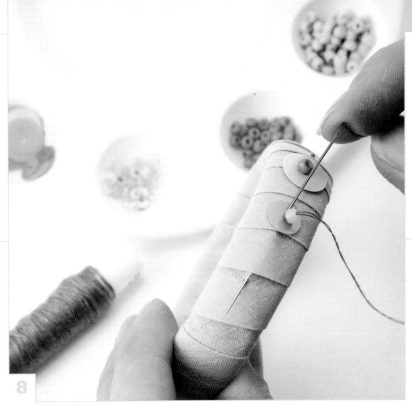

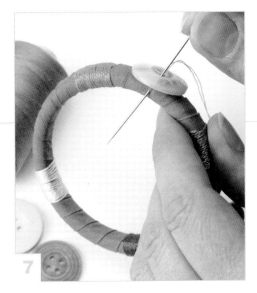

7 Using the hand-sewing needle and polyester sewing thread, sew on a large button in the four spaces between the wrapped sections. Bring the needle down the side of the bangle and through the bias binding to sew on each button.

8 Decorate the third bangle with beads and sequins. Using the beading needle and polyester sewing thread, make a firm backstitch in the binding where you want the first sequin to be. Bring the needle through the hole in the sequin then thread on a small bead. Bring the

needle back through the sequin and sew into the bias binding again, so that the bead holds the sequin in place. Bring the needle up through the bias binding at the next sequin position. Continue to stitch on sequins and beads around the circumference.

9 Finish by filling the remaining areas with small beads, making stitches under the bias binding until the next bead position is reached. Secure the thread with several firm stitches on the inside of the bangle.

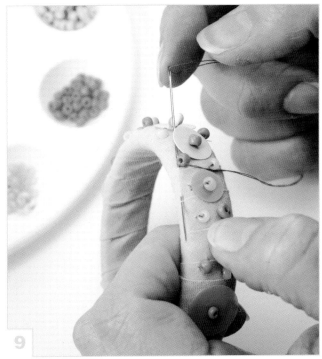

knitted corsage

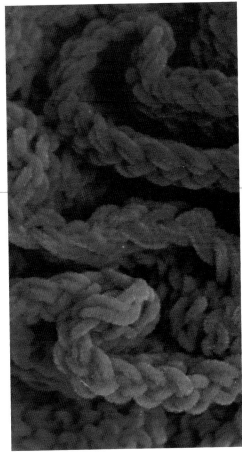

5 Turn each end of the stitched-together strips in opposite directions so that they lie flat against the underside of the flower. Stitch to the main body of the flower, again using overstitch.

6 Using the hand-sewing needle and polyester sewing thread, sew the brooch back finding to the back of the flower, slightly above the centre.

TIP THE IDEAS FOR KNITTED JEWELLERY ON PAGES 110–17 USE DIFFERENT PROCESSES AND A VARIETY OF MATERIALS. THEY CAN EASILY BE ADAPTED BY VARYING THE SCALE AND THE YARNS AND OTHER MATERIALS USED.

finger-knitted
necklace

FINGER KNITTING IS A SIMPLE AND fun way to produce pieces of jewellery such as bracelets and necklaces. Sequins and beads are threaded on to the wire and then incorporated as you knit. Think about using other materials to knit with, such as waxed cotton or silk thread from jewellery suppliers. You can also incorporate a variety of beads, buttons and other items into your piece.

As it's difficult to tell exactly how much wire you will need, it's a good idea to leave it on the spool until you have finished your knitting. The size of the stitches, and therefore the length of the knitting, will vary because of the varying size of fingers, so thread on a few more beads and sequins than you think you will need just in case you run out towards the end.

MATERIALS
- Approximately 2 m (78 in) of enamelled wire (1m (39 in) for a bracelet)
- 72 flower sequins of various sizes in pastel colours (36 for a bracelet)
- 234 small glass beads – with holes large enough to be threaded onto the wire (117 for a bracelet)
- 1 small button (optional for a bracelet)

EQUIPMENT
- Your fingers!
- Household scissors or wire cutters

1 Thread the sequins and beads onto the wire, threading on three beads between each sequin.

2 Continue until all the beads and sequins are used up.

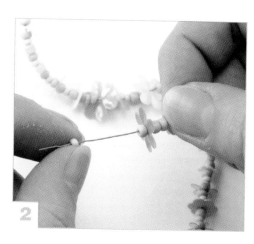

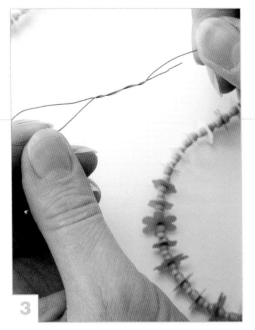

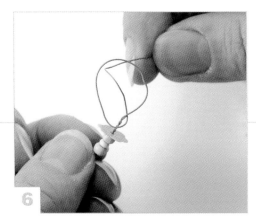

4 Fold the twisted wire over into a loop and thread the short end through the small loop. Twist the short end around the main length to secure the loop. This will form a loop for the fastening button, so check the size of both at this point and adjust if necessary.

5 Slip the first three beads and sequin down to the loop. Below them, make a loop in the wire.

6 Bend the main length of the wire through the first loop to form a slipknot. Place the slipknot over the forefinger of your left hand and pull firmly.

3 Fold over the last 10 cm (4 in) of the wire to make a loop. Twist the wires below the loop until you have a small loop remaining at one end and a length of wire measuring 3 cm (1¼ in) at the other, in addition to the main length of wire. (Be careful not to over twist the wire as it may break.)

variation

Included in the list of materials on page 114 are the numbers of beads and sequins and the length of wire required, to make an average sized finger-knit bracelet. Explore the range of sequins available on the internet: you can buy a surprising variety of qualities, shapes and colours.

9 Continue in this way until all the beads and sequins have been incorporated into the stitches. You should have 36 stitches, each containing six beads and two sequins. Hold the knitting around your neck to check the length.

Cut the wire with the scissors or wire cutters, leaving a 10 cm (4 in) tail. Bring the tail through the last loop and pull it tight to prevent the knitting unravelling.

10 Thread the tail of wire through the button and back again so the button is 2 cm (¾ in) from the end of the knitting. Twist the double strand of wire below the button, taking care not to over twist and trim off any excess.

7 Bring wire around your finger from front to back.

8 Using the thumb and forefinger of your right hand, lift the loop of wire to the left over the loop to the right and off your finger to form your first stitch. Slide the next six beads and two sequins down to your finger and make another stitch, incorporating the beads and sequins into it.

knitted
neckpiece

THIS METHOD OF MAKING AN
exciting, original yarn can be used to
make gorgeous jewellery, including this
dramatic neckpiece. Strips of fabric
are sewn together on a sewing
machine before being knitted up with
in garter stitch. Try making a head
band or colourful bracelets using the
same technique.

MATERIALS
- A selection of fine fabrics of
  various textures and qualities,
  such as silk dupion, organza
  and habotai
- Machine embroidery threads
  in toning colours, including a
  thicker one for the bobbin if
  wanted
- Matching polyester sewing
  threads

EQUIPMENT
- Fabric scissors or rotary
  cutter and cutting mat
- Sewing machine
- 8 mm (US size 11) knitting
  needles
- Hand-sewing needle
- Small, sharp embroidery
  scissors

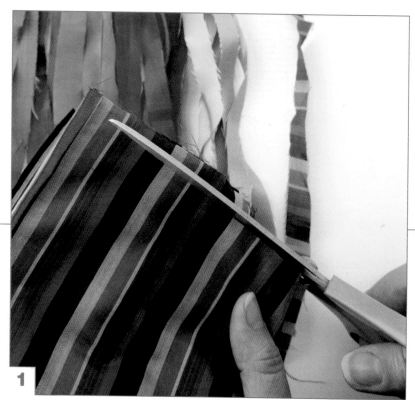

1 Using the fabric scissors or rotary cutter and cutting mat, cut the fabrics into strips measuring approximately 30 cm x 12 mm (12 x ½ in). You will need about 80 strips in total. Also cut about 80 strips measuring 10 cm x 12 mm (4 x ½ in). Cut a few extra strips of both lengths in case you need them.

2 Thread the sewing machine using embroidery thread on the top and thicker thread on the bobbin if you want (**see Using Thick Threads on the Bobbin, page 14**.) Place a

5

6

strip under the presser foot and using straight stitch, sew down the centre of it. When you are a short way from the end, overlap another strip in another colour and continue stitching. As you reach the halfway point along each strip, stop and lay a short strip at right angles across the main length, then sew over it.

3 Continue in this way until all the strips are used. Wind the strips into a ball of yarn.

4 Cast on 15 stitches using the newly made yarn.

5 Knit 40 rows to produce a piece of knitted fabric measuring approximately 50 cm (20 in) long. Check to make sure it fits comfortably around your neck and continue knitting if necessary. Cast off.

6 Lay the knitted strip flat, then make one twist in it.

7 Join the ends and, using the hand-sewing needle and polyester sewing thread, oversew them together.

7

templates

The templates are shown actual size unless otherwise stated. Where necessary, enlarge or reduce the templates on a photocopier by the percentages given. Make any necessary size adjustment, using tape to hold the pieces in place. Transfer the correct sized templates onto card. This will give you long-lasting templates that can be used again and again.

flower choker

page 18

orchid belt

page 22

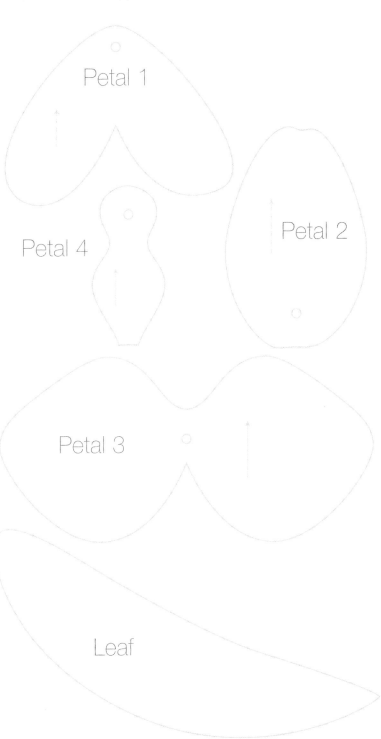

Petal 1

Petal 2

Petal 4

Petal 3

Leaf

filigree necklace
page 86

Enlarge by 50%

rose and diamanté corsage
page 70

Enlarge by 25%

dahlia corsage and cherry blossom earrings

pages 90 and 96

Enlarge both leaves by 25% for the Dahlia Corsage. Reduce the smaller leaf by 50% for the Cherry Blossom Earrings

Index

Page numbers in italics refer to illustrations. As many materials and techniques are used throughout the book, the page references are intended to direct the reader to substantial entries only.

author's
acknowledgements

THANKS TO:

- Lizzie Orme and Sussie Bell for the gorgeous pictures and for looking after us so well on the shoots.

- Elizabeth Healey for making the book look so beautiful.

- Janet Ravenscroft, Jane Birch, and all at Breslich & Foss for their support and advice and, most of all, their enthusiasm for my work.

- Lizzy and Mum for letting me raid your fabric stashes, button boxes, and wardrobes.

- My late Dad for recording our childhood in wonderful pictures that still evoke great memories.

- Steve, my lovely man, for all your support. Your cooking improves with every deadline crisis. Also, thanks for your expert knowledge of charity shops in Bristol and Bath.

Breslich and Foss Ltd would like to thank Kate Haxell for copy-editing the text and Stephen Dew for supplying the templates. Front cover image by the late Lindsay Stock.

DEDICATION

To Mum, sister Lizzy, and all my female friends who inspired the making of this book.